A Workbook of Ethical Case Scenarios in Applied Behavior
Analysis

Second Edition

A Workbook of Ethical Case Scenarios in Applied Behavior Analysis

Second Edition

DARREN J. SUSH

Department of Psychology, Pepperdine University, Los Angeles, CA, United States

ADEL C. NAJDOWSKI

Department of Psychology, Pepperdine University, Los Angeles, CA, United States

ACADEMIC PRESS

An imprint of Elsevier

Academic Press is an imprint of Elsevier
125 London Wall, London EC2Y 5AS, United Kingdom
525 B Street, Suite 1650, San Diego, CA 92101, United States
50 Hampshire Street, 5th Floor, Cambridge, MA 02139, United States
The Boulevard, Langford Lane, Kidlington, Oxford OX5 1GB, United Kingdom

Library of Congress Cataloging-in-Publication Data
A catalog record for this book is available from the Library of Congress

British Library Cataloguing-in-Publication Data
A catalogue record for this book is available from the British Library

ISBN 978-0-323-98813-1

For information on all Academic Press publications
visit our website at https://www.elsevier.com/books-and-journals

Publisher: Nikki Levy
Acquisitions Editor: Joslyn Chaiprasert-Paguio
Editorial Project Manager: Barbara Makinster
Production Project Manager: Punithavathy Govindaradjane
Cover Designer: Matthew Limbert

Typeset by STRAIVE, India
Transferred to Digital Printing 2021

CONTENTS

Chapter 6.

SECTION 2: RESPONSIBILITY IN PRACTICE   57

Chapter 7.

SECTION 3: RESPONSIBILITY TO CLIENTS AND STAKEHOLDERS   87

Chapter 8.

SECTION 4: RESPONSIBILITY TO SUPERVISEES AND TRAINEES   107

Chapter 9.

SECTION 5: RESPONSIBILITY IN PUBLIC STATEMENTS   117

ABOUT THE AUTHORS

Darren J. Sush, PsyD, BCBA-D (*he/him/his*), is a licensed clinical psychologist and a board certified behavior analyst (doctoral) with more than 15 years of experience developing and providing services based in Applied Behavior Analysis (ABA) for children and adults diagnosed with autism spectrum disorder (ASD) and developmental disabilities. Dr. Sush is Head of Autism and Psychology with Evernorth Behavioral Health, a Cigna corporation, and is the coauthor of *A Workbook of Ethical Case Scenarios in Applied Behavior Analysis*. He is an Adjunct Faculty member in the Applied Behavior Analysis program at Pepperdine University, and an Associate Professor in the Applied Behavior Analysis and Clinical Psychology programs at The Chicago School of Professional Psychology, teaching doctoral and master's courses in ABA and psychology. Within his practice, he has specialized in providing therapy for parents of children with ASD and developmental disabilities. He has also presented at regional and national conferences, has made appearances on several media outlets and podcasts, and has written for *Psychology Today* online, focusing on resources and mental health for parents of children with ASD and developmental disabilities.

Adel C. Najdowski, PhD, BCBA-D (*she/her/hers*), is an Associate Professor and the Director of the Master of Science in Applied Behavior Analysis (ABA) program at Pepperdine University as well as Research Manager at Halo Behavioral Health. Dr. Najdowski has provided ABA-based services to children with autism spectrum disorder (ASD) and developmental disabilities since 1995. She has more than 45 publications, including her books *Flexible and Focused: Teaching Executive Function Skills to Individuals With Autism and Attention Disorders* and *A Workbook of Ethical Case Scenarios in Applied Behavior Analysis*. She currently serves on the editorial board of the *Journal of Applied Behavior Analysis* and has previously served for *Behavior Analysis in Practice* and as Guest Editor for a special issue in *Research in Autism Spectrum Disorders*. She currently serves on the board of directors for the Behavior Analyst Certification Board (BACB) and previously served on the board of directors for the California Association for Behavior Analysis (CalABA). She is also on the disciplinary review committee (DRC) for the BACB. Her current research interests include topics related to social justice teaching higher-order skills to children, teens, and adults diagnosed with ASD. She is a frequent speaker at conferences and on podcasts and web-based shows.

DISCLAIMER

The content of this workbook is in no way affiliated with the Behavior Analyst Certification Board® (BACB®). All mentions of the BACB, Board Certified Behavior Analyst® (BCBA®), Board Certified Behavior Analyst-Doctoral™ (BCBA-D®), Board Certified Assistant Behavior Analyst® (BCaBA®), and Registered Behavior Technician® (RBT®) are owned and claimed by the BACB. The *Ethics Code for Behavior Analysts* (BACB, 2020) is the intellectual property of the BACB, and has been included with permission.

The opinions within this workbook, and responses provided within ethical case scenarios are not endorsed by the BACB and are solely the viewpoints of the authors. Case scenarios have been developed and generated as a means for promoting discussion and deliberation related to the ethical practice of behavior analysis.

Background and Preparation for Analysis of Ethical Case Scenarios

Chapter 1

A Brief Introduction to Ethics in Applied Behavior Analysis

Applied behavior analysis (ABA) is a rapidly growing field focusing on the application of principles of learning to better understand and improve behaviors of individuals, groups, and organizations to more appropriately and effectively achieve goals and develop socially significant behavior patterns (Baer et al., 1968; Cooper et al., 2020).

Though the work of most behavior analysts is focused on improving the lives of those impacted by their practice, most, if not all behavior analysts, potentially face ethical challenges on a daily basis. Such challenges may range from simple decisions regarding intervention implementation or inclusion of particular supports, to more precarious and complicated predicaments involving the health, safety, and well-being of the client (referred to as the "learner" in the remainder of this text), the family, or even the behavior analyst (Bailey & Burch, 2016).

The Behavior Analyst Certification Board's® (BACB®) *Ethics Code for Behavior Analysts* (see Appendix A) outlines six pertinent sections addressing the ethical practice of ABA and must be adhered to by all Board Certified Behavior Analysts® (BCBAs®), Board Certified Assistant Behavior Analysts® (BCaBAs®), and BACB applicants (BACB, 2020b). Similarly, the *RBTs® Ethics Code* (BACB, 2021) denotes ethical requirements for all Registered Behavior Technicians® and RBT applicants. For comprehensive information related to the development and application of the Code, as well as additional details regarding specific codes, we suggest reviewing the currently available text on this topic by Bailey and Burch (2016), as well as the updated edition not yet released at the time of this workbook.

A Workbook of Ethical Case Scenarios in Applied Behavior Analysis, Second Edition. https://doi.org/10.1016/B978-0-323-98813-1.00009-8

THE ROAD TO THE CODE

The development of the Code arose from the substantial and extended history of physical and mental abuse at the hands of some who associated themselves with the practice and implementation of the behavioral sciences. The victims of these abuses of power were very often those individuals whom the practitioner was meant to serve and support. Largely due to the resulting subjective productivity and progress, the stain associated with our related past was allowed to continue well beyond the point of reason (Bailey & Burch, 2016).

In response to these concerns, a standard of practice was developed by those who dedicated themselves to the advancement of the behavioral sciences and the application of knowledge and discovery to the betterment of society. Behavior analysts came to distinguish themselves from other clinicians and practitioners operating outside this approach and established more effective means for practitioners to communicate, share data, and distribute information.

A MODERN ETHICS CODE

While many behavior analysts have made substantial efforts to distance themselves and the field from morally and ethically problematic practices by championing efforts to support the rights, independence, and autonomy of the populations receiving services based in ABA (Leaf et al., 2021), it would be negligent and superficial to do so and not also acknowledge how the field of behavior analysis may have enabled, encouraged, or benefited from these harmful actions. As a result, behavior analysts must navigate both advancing the science and practice of the field and accepting the field's faults that have and continue to occur (Gershfeld Litvak & Sush, in press).

Since the initial development of standards for the ethical practice of behavior analysts, alterations and revisions have been made to parallel changing environments, expectations, and new revelations. The current version of the Code went into effect on January 1, 2022 (BACB, 2020b). Despite the inclusion of ethical issues most commonly experienced by behavior analysts and clear descriptions related to those concerns, ethical violations and risks of harm continue to occur. It is imperative that those practicing behavior analyses avoid presuming that because an ethical issue has been addressed within the Code, it no longer has the potential to transpire within everyday clinical practice (Dawson, 2004).

While the Code provides substantial guidance and direction, there remains a great deal of ambiguity, personal interpretation, and misunderstanding related to the ethical conduct of behavior analysts. Within the Code, the BACB has outlined specific and clear parameters, which an individual practicing behavior analysis can and should reference and follow. However, it is essentially impossible for the BACB to have included all situations and scenarios a behavior analyst may encounter when working within the field (Sellers et al., 2020). As a result, practicing behavior analysts must integrate their familiarity with the explicit expectations described in the Code with their own interpretations and their assessment of the particular clinical scenario. To this end, many behavior analysts can find themselves in an uncomfortable conflict as they attempt to integrate (1) their understanding of the Code, (2) their intention to provide what they believe to be the most beneficial intervention for learners, and (3) perhaps, their own best interests.

THE CONTINUED STUDY OF ETHICS

Coursework and practical experience related to the ethical practice of behavior analysis are currently well integrated within most ABA-based graduate training programs. The BACB publishes a task-list (BACB, 2017) from which all those interested in sitting for the BACB's certification exam must receive training via coursework and supervised experience hours. While there may be a "learn by doing" component incorporated within much of the work demonstrated by a behavior analyst, along with coursework in foundation, theory, and practice, ethics within ABA may be less amenable to such strategies. Simply working within the field, even when supervised by a well-seasoned practitioner, does not guarantee that a behavior analyst will be prepared for all of the ethical challenges they will likely encounter. As such, it is imperative for behavior analysts not only to rely on the knowledge gained from their supervisor and their own supervised clinical experience but also to be exposed to a wider variety of ethical challenges both within their formal educational experience and during continuing education following certification (Handelsman, 1986).

Despite their best efforts to be well educated and well informed in the ethical practice of behavior analysis, certified individuals must be cautious to avoid a false sense of ethical competence and confidence. "Acting ethically" (as broad a term as that admittedly may be) is often not solely the result of having knowledge in the most appropriate course of action but also includes the awareness of one's own limitations for determining the multitude of risks and benefits associated with those potential courses of action (Ghezzi & Rehfeldt, 1994).

Practitioners may encounter situations in which following the specific direction of the Code does not appear to be in the best interest of the learner. As a result, behavior analysts are tasked with the extremely difficult charge of remaining adherent to pertinent sections of the Code while also assessing deviations to minimize the potential for harm (Sellers et al., 2020). Unfortunately, no amount of coursework or supervised experience can comprehensively prepare a behavior analyst for these situations.

However, this does not necessarily mean that behavior analysts are thereby expected to fulfill the impossible task of "knowing what they do not know" and thereby independently meeting an ideal standard. While it may be true that an ethically challenging scenario could potentially arise at any moment within a behavior analyst's career, the professional should not resign to this inevitability and forgo any responsibility for preparation or prevention. Conversely, it is not feasible for behavior analysts to function in a manner in which the anticipation of an ethical pitfall becomes so paramount that their clinical effectiveness or willingness to participate within the field wanes.

Ethical practice often directly coincides with clinically effective practice. Though there is always potential for ethical conflicts, the vast majority of situations within which a behavior analyst will practice will not result in debate or concern. Most challenging ethical scenarios, even those that seem to arise without warning, often result from a progression that can be identified with a careful retrospective review (Smith, 2003). Hindsight provides a clearer picture of the evolution of the ethically challenging scenario and the factors that likely contributed to its development and maintenance.

ANALYZING ETHICAL CHALLENGES

Behavior analysts are adept at the assessment of the events occurring both before and following a targeted behavior. Our skills in this area can be directly applied to the behaviors associated with an ethically difficult situation. By reviewing the antecedents leading to the incident, behavior analysts may better prepare themselves for the avoidance of future ethical problems. Additionally, as behavior analysts incorporate a more proactive approach toward ethical understanding and identification, practitioners may become more proficient at identifying situations that could potentially lead to an ethical issue and avoid the occurrence of a violation. In order for practicing behavior analysts to be successful in either preventing or remediating ethical damages, they must identify their contributions to the scenario, skill and proficiency in managing the scenario, and willingness to diverge or correct the progression of the situation (Bailey & Burch, 2016).

In some cases, behavior analysts may encounter scenarios within their professional practice during which engaging in a particular strategy may not follow the specifications of the established Code but instead may arguably be of increased benefit to the behavior analyst. As with any other behavior, ethical behavior by behavior analysts is reinforced and thereby continued (Brodhead & Higbee, 2012). However, the contingencies in place maintaining ethical behavior may compete with the immediate or more highly valued contingencies potentially available for engagement in unethical behavior. The behavior analyst may find it more personally beneficial to engage in unethical practice than to follow the specifications identified within the Code. Adding to this, there is no real assurance that the unethical practices exhibited by a behavior analyst will be discovered and result in consequences to impede similar unethical behavior in the future (Sellers et al., 2016a). Such circumstances may become even more complicated when potentially unethical actions of the behavior analyst also happen to have a direct clinical benefit for the learner or the clinical relationship.

The imbalance between the impetus to practice ethically and engage in unethical behavior, the confusion when ethical stipulations interfere with clinical rationale, the potential to misinterpret or misconstrue ethical codes, the ambiguity of ethical actions, and the lack of experience in all prospective ethical scenarios, may leave a behavior analyst feeling unprepared, unsupported, and vulnerable. However, there are strategies that can assist in increasing the likelihood of ethical action and reducing ethical pitfalls.

In addition to participating in ethical coursework while in a graduate training program and continuing education following certification, behavior analysts can encourage the continued study of ethics among their colleagues and within their professional organizations. Companies may benefit from establishing an ethics coordinator to oversee the distribution of ethical training, information, and guidance. Such a coordinator could also act as a source of advice for other members of the organization who may encounter an ethical challenge (Brodhead & Higbee, 2012). Agencies may also benefit from the establishment of an ethics committee to assist in addressing ethical concerns and promote understanding through multiple viewpoints, opinions, and resources (Cox, 2020).

If such resources are not formally available within an ABA-based organization, or when the behavior analyst operates as an independent practitioner, it may still be possible to seek out colleagues to discuss ethical conflicts and determine appropriate responses (Smith, 2003). Perhaps the most advantageous strategy for avoiding or managing ethically precarious situations is for the behavior analysts to take the appropriate actions to be familiar with the Code and its content areas so that they may more easily reference potential problems and identify challenges before they escalate (Bailey & Burch, 2016).

Some areas of the Code are significantly more commonplace than others. It is likely impossible to accurately determine the aspects of the Code that are most frequently violated or those areas of the Code that practitioners may encounter on a more regular basis, as most ethical code challenges and violations go unreported. Yet, if behavior analysts are practicing within the field for long enough, they will likely either directly encounter or be made aware of an ethical challenge involving (1) multiple relationships, (2) issues related to confidentiality, (3) challenges in the supervisory experience, (4) questions related to working within their clinical expertise and competence, (5) establishing and discontinuing the clinical relationship, and (6) the influx and inclusion of alternative or supplemental treatment strategies (Smith, 2003).

According to the Behavior Analyst Certification Board (2018), the three most frequent ethical challenges reported and determined to be a violation since the previous Code went into effect on January 1, 2016, were (1) issues related to supervision, (2) reporting and responding to ethical challenges, and (3) professionalism and integrity. Developing an awareness of these ethical challenges can help a behavior analyst not only better identify problematic situations and prepare for their potential likelihood but also ideally prevent and avoid their occurrence (Britton et al., 2021).

While some ethical challenges occur more frequently than others, not all ethical issues require the same depth of response or hold the same inherent risk of harm. Though behavior analysts likely will not have a solution to every ethical issue they may possibly encounter at any time, it does not mean that those practicing within the field cannot or should not be prepared with an appropriate strategy for addressing ethical issues should a challenging situation occur. A behavior analyst's experience and preparation, along with the complexity of the ethical dilemma, play vital roles in their competence for managing these ethical scenarios in a safe and appropriate manner that minimizes the potential for future damage. Bailey and Burch (2016) outline strategies for identifying complex ethical situations and assessing appropriate responses. Ethical scenarios may be considered more complex when (1) they encompass multiple areas of the Code, (2) more than one person is involved, (3) the ethical violation is less clear or straightforward, and (4) there is a risk to the learner or the behavior analyst. In response, Bailey and Burch suggest recruiting assistance from more proficient practitioners should the ethical situation be beyond the expertise of the individual behavior analyst.

Once a situation has been identified as problematic, the behavior analyst should first identify if the issue is actually covered within the Code. After which, the behavior analyst may then identify all the individuals and parties that may be affected by the ethical concern and develop a plan for addressing the issue with strategies for barriers to implementation, follow-up measures, and documentation (BACB, 2020b; Bailey & Burch, 2016; Forester-Miller & Davis, 2016).

Chapter 2

Using This Workbook

The purpose of this workbook is to allow users the opportunity to work through ethical scenarios that could potentially occur during practice as behavior analysts. The intent is to facilitate the development of a repertoire for recognizing ethically concerning situations and engaging in ethically appropriate solution-focused problem-solving. Given this, the focus of this workbook is on providing example case scenarios of various ethical situations that may be commonly encountered during the career of a behavior analyst. Chapter 3, Suggestions for Ethical Decision-Making, provides suggestions to consider when making ethical decisions. Chapter 4, Examples of Completed Case Scenarios, provides two examples of case scenarios that have been evaluated and addressed. Chapters 5–10 correspond with the six sections of the Code. Within the scenarios presented in these chapters, a primary ethical violation may be identified relating to the overall subject of the chapter. Chapter 11, Complex Scenarios Involving Multiple Sections of the Code, includes more complicated scenarios in which significant components of multiple sections of the Code may be directly involved.

As with most real-world ethical challenges, the case scenarios presented may represent ethical violations in one or multiple areas of the Code. While some scenarios may present dilemmas that are clear violations, others may include situations that are not a violation of the Code as presented, but instead may relate to a particular code. Some scenarios have also been included to highlight situations that may potentially result in a violation if not appropriately addressed.

In order to best integrate the unique challenges and needs of those teaching, practicing, or learning applied behavior analysis (ABA), cases range in difficulty, complexity, and risk to the behavior analyst, the behavior analytic community, the learner, or other parties related to the learner. Following each case scenario, questions are provided to assist in understanding the Code and driving contemplation and discussion.

Keeping with the suggested models for ethical decision-making and analysis described earlier (BACB, 2020b; Bailey & Burch, 2016; Forester-Miller & Davis, 2016), you are asked to first carefully review the provided case scenario by highlighting crucial elements related to the Code, the clinical and professional factors identified, and any potential risk or harm to those involved.

Once recognized, you should compare the key elements of the case scenario with the Code. At this point, it may be beneficial to differentiate actions that appear to be in clear violation of the Code versus elements of the scenario that are not yet an infraction but are an area of concern or necessary focus. Through comparison of the scenario and the Code, it may then be beneficial to describe the reasons each element of the Code was identified and why you believe a violation did or did not occur.

A Workbook of Ethical Case Scenarios in Applied Behavior Analysis, Second Edition. https://doi.org/10.1016/B978-0-323-98813-1.00002-5

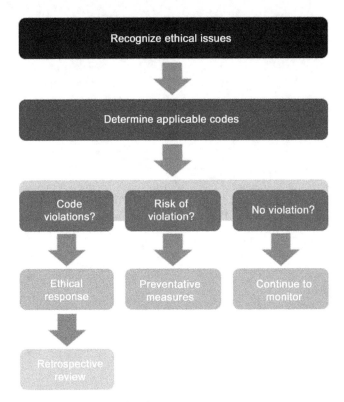

Figure 2.1 Suggested flowchart for analyzing ethical scenarios.

To obtain a clear understanding of the problematic situation and ideally prevent future challenges, a thorough analysis of the antecedent and consequent events related to the scenario should be conducted. You may then illustrate the possible course of events that might have led to the ethical challenge and what actions the individual(s) identified within the scenario could have taken to prevent the scenario from occurring. In addition, actions the individual(s) within the scenario should complete as a result of the presented challenge to minimize risk, prevent further escalation, and/or resolve decision-making should be described (Fig. 2.1).

Many of the ethical scenarios provide specific critical thinking questions related to the case or the associated codes to help facilitate further discussion and understanding. You are encouraged to develop your own additional critical thinking questions and potential answers.

Suggestions of ethics codes that relate to each scenario are presented (Appendix B). It should be noted that there may be additional codes that relate to the scenario, and the recommended code(s) is only the opinion of the current authors. As a result, users of this workbook are encouraged to first determine their own impressions of related ethics code(s) for each scenario prior to accessing the available suggestions to minimize potential bias. Additionally, while the authors of this workbook may believe a particular code may be considered most relevant, these suggestions should not be interpreted as the sole "correct" response, as there is a significant possibility that with further analysis and discussion, alternative or additional codes may be considered equally or more appropriate. Finally, the authors have been careful not to include all of the potential identified codes for each scenario to assist in the facilitation of discussion, interpretation, and analysis by the user of this workbook.

Chapter 3

Suggestions for Ethical Decision-Making

In this workbook, scenarios representing ethical challenges commonly encountered by practicing behavior analysts or those studying within the field are provided. As has been discussed, the likelihood of engaging in ethical behavior is increased when one is not only familiar with and understands the Code but can also identify and apply strategies meant to prevent ethical challenges from potentially deteriorating into clear violations or situations that would result in the potential harm of those involved.

Ethics codes can be leveraged as resources for boosting appropriate and adaptive management of potential ethical issues when they are accessed as a proactive opportunity instead of simply a set of rules for determining the need for disciplinary action or judging mistakes and transgressions (Gershfeld Litvak & Sush, in press).

While a proactive approach toward the prevention of unethical behavior may be ideal, it is likely impossible to circumvent the inevitability of ethical dilemmas. As a result, it is important for practicing behavior analysts to identify a reliable and comfortable strategy for managing an ethical problem. Following each ethical scenario presented within this workbook, you are asked to address and identify your thoughts toward the most appropriate subsequent course of action of individuals involved within the given example, with reference to the Code.

There are multiple suggested approaches in standardizing ethical decision-making within the field of applied behavior analysis (ABA; BACB, 2020b; Bailey & Burch, 2016). While there are slight variations in the order of tactics to consider, most recommendations for analyzing ethical issues follow the general strategies outlined below. For a more comprehensive discussion of the implications of ethical challenges within the field and practical tactics of ethical problem-solving, we suggest reviewing the text, *Practical Ethics for Effective Treatment of Autism Spectrum Disorder* by Brodhead, et al. (2018a) on the subject, which is scheduled to have an updated edition not yet released at the time of writing this workbook.

Practitioners and students may benefit from approaching the question of how to proceed following an ethically difficult situation (like those provided within this workbook) by first following these suggestions:

1. Reference the Code to determine if there are any clear directions or descriptions that relate to the given scenario.
2. Identify areas of the Code that may relate to the scenario but do not provide clear or sufficient guidance.
3. Review the Code for areas that may appear to provide conflicting direction.
4. Ask yourself how you might resolve any conflicts within the Code or gather additional necessary information to use within your decision-making.
5. Recognize future ethical implications or risks that might occur should no corrective action or changes in the procedure be taken by individuals involved.

A Workbook of Ethical Case Scenarios in Applied Behavior Analysis, Second Edition. https://doi.org/10.1016/B978-0-323-98813-1.00014-1

Once you have sufficiently addressed the areas above, it may be helpful to move forward by asking yourself the following questions:

1. Given the ethical codes that I have already identified as relating to the scenario, what do I believe is the most ethical course of action to either repair the situation or prevent further escalation?
2. Given my chosen course of action, what might be the risk of harm to the learner, myself, collateral individuals, and/or the environment?
3. What should I continue to monitor or be aware of to mitigate additional harm or ethical challenges moving forward?

With the release of the most recent code, the BACB (2020b) suggests approaching each ethical dilemma by focusing on the details of the scenario itself and whether the situation does, in fact, pose an ethical concern. Identifying the parties involved and the potential impact to each individual, as well as any possibility of harm as a result of the situation or response, is an important next step. Seeking support and consultation throughout may assist behavior analysts in exploring helpful solutions. As the behavior analyst's understanding of these factors will be highly influenced by their own priorities and potential biases, it is necessary and important to identify personal values that may impact how one addresses the dilemma and chooses to resolve the concern. Finally, documenting decisions and results may assist in avoiding further escalation, while also potentially preventing similar circumstances from reaching challenging levels in the future.

While following this suggested approach may be beneficial when addressing the ethical scenarios presented in this workbook, there may not be a single best response when encountering real-life ethical challenges. Though the Code may be clearly defined, each individual may identify different priorities within an ethical challenge based on the context surrounding the situation.

The circumstances contributing to ethical challenges can and should remain the primary factors influencing the identification of ethical issues and corrective actions; however, it is equally important for behavior analysts to acknowledge the impact of their own training and expertise in responding to and managing ethical challenges in general and under similar conditions (Handelsman, 1986). Reactions toward ethical dilemmas may be influenced by the behavior analyst's identification and resolution of their own personal investment in the outcome or progression of the ethical issue (Gershfeld Litvak & Sush, in press). When faced with opportunities to respond to ethical problems, behavior analysts must be aware of the factors influencing their motivation for particular outcomes and ensure the client's best interest remain a priority (Sellers et al., 2016a). A behavior analyst's recognition of factors influencing ethically precarious circumstances, the identification of relevant and related ethics codes, and determination of how best to manage or resolve the issue may be most highly determined by the behavior analyst's own morals, values, and personal beliefs. The cultural foundation, history, and background of the behavior analyst may set a framework for interpreting ethical issues and decision-making (Brodhead, 2019; Rosenberg & Schwartz, 2019). Understanding the importance and potential influence of these factors may better serve learners, our field, and ourselves in approaching ethical challenges with the same level of analysis, interest, and investigation that behavior analysts approach targeted challenging behaviors.

Chapter 4

Examples of Completed Case Scenarios

The case scenarios contained in this workbook are meant to assist those studying and practicing applied behavior analysis (ABA) to better identify and manage ethically challenging situations. Subsequent chapters of this workbook provide examples of ethical dilemmas potentially encountered by those practicing within the field as they relate to the Code. Following each case scenario, several questions are provided to encourage reflection and discussion. Two completed examples of such deliberation are provided within this chapter to illustrate and guide the analysis of ethical predicaments in ABA.

The answers provided may not be the only available explanation but rather examples of potential responses. As with the case scenarios detailed later in this workbook, you are encouraged to engage in your own analysis and determine your own solutions.

A Workbook of Ethical Case Scenarios in Applied Behavior Analysis, Second Edition. https://doi.org/10.1016/B978-0-323-98813-1.00016-5

Joaquin is a newly certified behavior analyst. He works at an agency with several other Board Certified Behavior Analysts (BCBAs) and a few senior clinicians. Each year, a few of the BCBAs attend the regional ABA conference, and usually, one or two will attend a national or international conference. Though Joaquin would like to join them, his office does not cover the cost of travel or the conference registration fee, and he is not able to afford to take time off of work or pay to attend on his own. As a result, Joaquin does not make any effort to gain more information or experience. Since he is newly certified, he feels confident that the strategies based in ABA he was taught in graduate school and during supervision are sufficient.

Applicable Ethics Code(s):	1.06: Maintaining Competence			
Rationale for Chosen Code(s):				
Joaquin may be in danger of violating code 1.06, as it is a behavior analyst's ethical responsibility to continue to maintain their professional development beyond their initial school experience and supervised training. I do not think there is a violation just yet, since Joaquin still has an opportunity to gain relevant experience and education.				
Code Violation?	Yes	No	Need More Information	(If Situation Continues)
Antecedent Factors Contributing to Scenario:				
Joaquin has not yet violated the Code. However, the lack of understanding of his ethical responsibility to maintain his professional development likely contributed to his misunderstanding related to his training obligations.				
Preventative Strategies:				
Being more familiar with the Code may have helped to prevent Joaquin's inaccurate perception. Additionally, he could have approached his agency to arrange alternative means for gaining continued development such as hosting an agency journal club.				
Ethical Course of Action:				
Joaquin should identify alternative ways to maintain competence.				
Future Risk Factors to Keep in Mind:				
Without continued education, he may miss opportunities to further develop his skills and competence as a behavior analyst and have less awareness of updates and advancements in the field.				
Discussion Questions:				
Besides attending conferences, how else might Joaquin maintain competence and continue his professional development?				
Joaquin can maintain competence by:				

Joaquin can maintain competence by:

1. listening to recorded presentations from conferences
2. subscribing to journals and reading research articles
3. attending local workshops
4. attending online continuing education seminars and workshops
5. listening to podcasts on the topic of ABA
6. taking additional behavior-analytic courses

TAKING TESTIMONIALS

Nita is updating the website of her agency that practices ABA. She has included all of her agency's services, contact information, logos, and graphics. Despite including several pages to inform potential clients about ABA and her agency's intervention focus, she wants to put a more personal touch on the website that will allow those searching for services to gain a more direct understanding of her agency. Nita has approached a few of the parents of the learners she serves to ask if they would be willing to provide a short description of the services they receive or an anonymous quote about their satisfaction with the agency and staff. One parent said that she would be more than happy to provide an endorsement for the website, especially if Nita is able to switch back a staff member who was recently removed from her son's team due to a scheduling conflict.

Applicable Ethics Code(s):	5.07: Soliciting Testimonials from Current Clients for Advertising	1.13: Coercive and Exploitative Relationships		
Rationale for Chosen Code(s):				
Approaching the parents of current learners and asking if they would be willing to write a comment or endorsement for her agency's website is a direct violation of code 5.07, which states that behavior analysts are not to request testimonials from current clients. Requesting the testimonial increases Nita's risk of engaging in a coercive and exploitative relationship with the learner's parents as described in code 1.13. Nita puts herself and the learner's parent in an uncomfortable and challenging position in which the learner's parent may feel obligated to provide a positive endorsement in exchange for continued service, and in this case, having the preferred staff member returned to the team. In this situation, Nita is in control of the content of her website, and she is not simply responding to unsolicited claims that may have been posted on an online review website that she does not manage. I do not believe that code 5.08 is applicable in this situation as Nita is specifically requesting endorsements from current clients and there is no indication she has contacted former clients. If this was the case, she would need to include whether the testimonial was solicited or not. I also do not believe code 5.09 is applicable in this situation as Nita's company's website would be considered a form of advertisement for the purposes of promoting her agency.				
Code Violation?	(Yes)	No	Need More Information	If Situation Continues
Antecedent Factors Contributing to Scenario:				
Nita has the option of including testimonials from former clients on her website as long as these testimonials are clearly indicated as having been solicited. If Nita does access testimonials from former clients, she should be aware of the continued risk that may be involved regarding her relationship with the former clients, any potential for return to services, and disclosure of personal information.				
Preventative Strategies:				
Nita could have avoided the ethical violation had she not requested the testimonials from the learner's parents. She could have explored other options for increasing the personal nature of her website, such as including her agency's mission statement, her own professional bio, and reasons for working within the field of ABA.				

Ethical Course of Action:

Since Nita has already approached the learner's parents asking for their testimonials, it is now her responsibility to repair the violation to the best of her ability. She could speak with all the parents she requested testimonials from and inform them that she made a mistake in asking for their quotes, as this is a violation of the Code. She can also inform the specific parent who asked for the staffing change that her agency does their best to provide the best staff for the learners they work with, and she can make a note to look at the particular staff's availability; however, she is not able to change the schedule because of the requested endorsement.

Future Risk Factors to Keep in Mind:

Nita will likely have to continue to be prepared for parents to potentially make similar requests as the parent described in the scenario.

Nita could also gain more personal continuing education and promote additional staff training in her agency focused on ethics in behavior analysis.

Discussion Questions:

What might you take into consideration if Nita approached former clients for statements on her website rather than current clients?

The Code allows for testimonials to be requested and included on agency websites from former clients. However, it must be clearly identified whether the testimonial was solicited or unsolicited and must also include a description of the relationship between the individual who wrote the testimonial and the behavior analyst. Requesting and including testimonials from former clients may still raise ethical concerns that behavior analysts must continue to monitor. For example, former clients may request to return to participating in services, which may impact the reestablished therapeutic relationship or may make them feel obligated to provide a positive statement.

Ethical Case Scenarios

Chapter 5

Section 1: Responsibility as a Professional

Although the field of applied behavior analysis (ABA) has grown exponentially in recent years, with an increase of almost 450% in the last 10 years alone as of the time this book was written (BACB, n.d.), we are still a relatively young community of professionals. In fact, approximately 50% of all current certificants were certified in the last 5 years—a proportion that is expected to continue to rise. As such, our reputation both within and outside our field is yet to be fully solidified and remains subject to interpretation by others if we do not establish and maintain its identity for ourselves.

Perhaps one of the greatest challenges to preserving our identity as behavior analysts is the ethically questionable behavior of those who continue to be associated with our field. It may be easy for an ethical behavior analyst to view "behavior modifiers" with disdain and distance ourselves as completely separate practitioners of the greater good. Yet, the fact remains that the history of our field is relatively short, and the ethical challenges associated with the history of the behavioral sciences are proportionately recent. Thus, these events are not only fresh in the minds of the communities with whom we wish to serve or collaborate, but unfortunately, they may still continue to occur.

Many people, even those within the healthcare, mental health, human resources, and organizational fields, endorse a strongly held negative opinion of the field of ABA (Leaf et al., 2021). Therefore, the responsibility of each individual who identifies themselves as a behavior analyst is significant and substantial.

While we as a field may be more aware of the repercussions, societal impact, and systemic implications of the ethical issues that occurred, it is important to also acknowledge how these practices may have helped form the course and direction of the profession as it is practiced today. The increase in professionals gaining experience and joining the field of behavior analysis provides an opportunity to engage in introspection, to learn from past transgressions, attempt to understand, recognize and comprehend contributing factors that may still be present, and focus on promoting and establishing meaningful change (Gershfeld Litvak & Sush, in press).

The increase in those pursuing careers in behavior analysis may create significantly greater access to intervention and services based in ABA for those who may not have otherwise had the opportunity to connect with knowledgeable and trained professionals. Similarly, the growth of the field may result in increased capability to share information with colleagues, may lead to more individuals dedicated to advancing the science and practice of behavior analysis, and further dissemination of the benefits of ABA to the public. However, as with any development and progress, behavior analysts must also be cognizant of the increased risk associated with the rapid growth and newly found popularity of the field. As more new professionals enter into the workforce, interact with the public, and provide services for organizations and learners, the probability of ethical issues, challenges, and problems escalates.

As a behavior analyst, personally performing well within one's professional role will hopefully have a promising reflection on their career. However, perhaps because of the (a) short tenure of our field, (b) uncertainty across communities about our foundations and practices, and (c) regrettable actions and reputation related to our past, the unethical behavior of even just one member of our community could have a large and lasting impact across the entire field.

Considering the importance and the accountability that each individual behavior analyst holds, not only for themselves but also for the field as a whole, the BACB Ethics Code (BACB, 2020b) begins with Section 1 by addressing the responsibility of behavior analysts as professionals. The elements within this section of the Code dictate the expectations, standards, and ideals for the professional practice of behavior analysts. Responsible behavior analysts must not only conduct themselves in a manner that reflects positively on themselves but also facilitates the public's understanding and perception of the field's values and ethical priorities.

Highlighted within Section 1 is the importance of maintaining professional competence, which may be achieved through engaging in professional development, attending conferences, accessing relevant literature, and receiving supervision and mentorship, as well as several other valuable activities. Competence may be referred to as performing the roles and tasks associated with being a professional behavior analyst in a manner that may be considered proficient and capable based on a set of criteria (Brodhead et al., 2018b). While maintaining professional competence may establish a baseline standard of expectation, ethical behavior analysts may avoid only striving toward mediocrity by understanding their own boundaries and limitations (Ghezzi & Rehfeldt, 1994). Responsible behavior analysts will identify areas where they do not have an appropriate skill set from which to work independently and will either refer to other professionals or seek supervision as appropriate.

With this in mind, the Code further establishes professional competence to include the application of research-based, behavioral strategies and principles, as well as the knowledge and skill related to the individualized impact of the behavior analyst's relationship and involvement with those who receive services based in ABA. Behavior analysts must be aware of their own personal biases and ability to be responsive to individuals with diverse backgrounds and needs. As behavior analysts' morals, values, and learning history may impact their understanding and interpretation of the Code, professionals must also consider how these beliefs may influence their interaction with organizations and learners receiving their support (Brodhead, 2019; Rosenberg & Schwartz, 2019). Awareness, education, and integration of the cultural values, beliefs, and preferences of learners, families, and groups participating in provided services will assist behavior analysts in establishing proficiency and competence as a practitioner across diverse individuals. Cultural responsiveness and attentiveness may assist practicing behavior analysts to conduct more meaningful data collection and establish more impactful, individualized, and conscious intervention strategies (Fong et al., 2016). For comprehensive and valuable insight into developing cultural responsiveness as a behavior analyst, we suggest reviewing the Multicultural Alliance of Behavior Analysis's Proposed *Standards for Cultural Competence in Behavior Analysis* by Fong and Tanaka (2013).

CASE 1: SIGNED, SEALED

After completing all of her supervised experience hours, Kiera has officially been promoted at an agency that practices ABA. She is confident that she will pass her upcoming Board Certified Behavior Analyst (BCBA) exam. With her new position comes increased responsibilities, an increased salary, and a company email account. In keeping with agency standards, Kiera creates a signature line to go on the bottom of her emails providing her name, followed by "BCBA Candidate."

Applicable Ethics Code(s):				
Rationale for Chosen Code(s):				
Code Violation?	Yes	No	Need More Information	If Situation Continues
Antecedent Factors Contributing to Scenario:				
Preventative Strategies:				
Ethical Course of Action:				
Future Risk Factors to Keep in Mind:				

CASE 2: LICENSED TO ILL

Andrew is a BCBA who practices in a state that offers licensure for behavior analysts. While he has maintained his continuing education and renewal requirements for his BCBA, he has missed the designated deadline for maintaining his licensure status. Andrew continues to give out his old business cards indicating his credentials as "BCBA, LBA."

Applicable Ethics Code(s):				
Rationale for Chosen Code(s):				
Code Violation?	Yes	No	Need More Information	If Situation Continues
Antecedent Factors Contributing to Scenario:				
Preventative Strategies:				
Ethical Course of Action:				
Future Risk Factors to Keep in Mind:				

CASE 3: DROPPED DEADLINE

Talia is a BCBA providing ABA services for Inez as funded through the school district. Inez's Individual Education Plan (IEP) meeting is scheduled for this coming Monday. As noted in her contracting agreement, each member of the IEP team is asked to complete a formal IEP goal progress report prior to the meeting. Talia forgot to obtain Inez's data book and will now be unable to complete her report and updates in time for the meeting. Talia plans to inform Inez's parents and the IEP team about the mistake and give a general update on progress at the meeting and submit her formal report later if requested.

Applicable Ethics Code(s):				
Rationale for Chosen Code(s):				
Code Violation?	Yes	No	Need More Information	If Situation Continues
Antecedent Factors Contributing to Scenario:				
Preventative Strategies:				
Ethical Course of Action:				
Future Risk Factors to Keep in Mind:				

CASE 4: DIVIDED ATTENTION

Monique, a BCBA, is providing direct supervision of a Registered Behavior Technician (RBT) and a learner, Sophia, within the school setting. The classroom is made up of both typically developing students and those with behavioral supports. Another student who is not receiving services from Monique's agency, Jameson, has a direct behavior aide who is running late and will not be at the school for at least another 2 hours. Jameson's frequent challenging behavior is disrupting the rest of the class. Since Sophia is already receiving direct support from the RBT from Monique's agency, the teacher asks Monique if she is available to assist with Jameson until the behavior aide arrives.

Applicable Ethics Code(s):				
Rationale for Chosen Code(s):				
Code Violation?	Yes	No	Need More Information	If Situation Continues
Antecedent Factors Contributing to Scenario:				
Preventative Strategies:				
Ethical Course of Action:				
Future Risk Factors to Keep in Mind:				
Discussion Questions:				
What are the ethical implications if Monique assists with Jameson?				
Does Monique have any ethical or clinical obligations to the teacher and Jameson?				

CASE 5: PARENTS' NIGHT OUT

Marcella is an RBT working at an agency that practices ABA. She received a call from her cousin stating that she has a friend with a son diagnosed with autism spectrum disorder (ASD). The child's parents are looking to hire a caretaker who can provide support and "babysitting" services in the home while they run errands in the community or spend time together out of the house. The parents are looking for someone who has experience working with children diagnosed with ASD and may be more familiar with their son's communication capabilities and behaviors.

Applicable Ethics Code(s):				
Rationale for Chosen Code(s):				
Code Violation?	Yes	No	Need More Information	If Situation Continues
Antecedent Factors Contributing to Scenario:				
Preventative Strategies:				
Ethical Course of Action:				
Future Risk Factors to Keep in Mind:				
Discussion Questions:				
Would your advice to Marcella change if, while "babysitting," the family was also interested in Marcella providing behavioral support and intervention based in ABA? What additional/alternative ethics codes might apply if this was the situation, if any?				
Would your advice to Marcella change if instead of a friend of Marcella's cousin, the request to provide "babysitting" services came from a former learner that worked with Marcella at the ABA agency? What if the request was from a current learner? What additional/alternative ethics codes might apply if this was the situation, if any?				

CASE 6: RISKY REFERRAL

Kylie has worked in the field for several years as a BCBA supervising and developing ABA programs for young children (ages 2–8) diagnosed with ASD. She received a referral for a new case who is a 16-year-old girl with a diagnosis of obsessive–compulsive disorder (OCD). Within her work, Kylie has used ABA strategies to reduce ritualistic and repetitive behaviors and increase flexibility and tolerance.

Applicable Ethics Code(s):				
Rationale for Chosen Code(s):				
Code Violation?	Yes	No	Need More Information	If Situation Continues
Antecedent Factors Contributing to Scenario:				
Preventative Strategies:				
Ethical Course of Action:				
Future Risk Factors to Keep in Mind:				
Discussion Questions:				
How might you suggest Kylie proceed if she was informed that no other local BCBAs were available to assist with the new referral?				

CASE 7: LEARN SOMETHING NEW

Lena is a BCBA who has just returned from attending a national ABA conference. Among the many symposia and panel sessions she attended, Lena was particularly impressed by a presentation focused on the applicability and use of a validated assessment tool in determining progress and assisting with intervention planning. The discussion reviewed the assessment tool, its use and application, and provided information on administration and scoring. Upon returning from the conference, Lena discovered that the most recent copy of the assessment tool, as well as the scoring manual and administration sheets, are in her agency's library. Thinking it would be helpful for a new case, she uses the assessment tool to conduct the intake, establish baseline measures, and develop goals.

Applicable Ethics Code(s):				
Rationale for Chosen Code(s):				
Code Violation?	Yes	No	Need More Information	If Situation Continues
Antecedent Factors Contributing to Scenario:				
Preventative Strategies:				
Ethical Course of Action:				
Future Risk Factors to Keep in Mind:				

Carlos is a recently certified BCBA looking for a new job. He interviewed at a company that states on their website that they provide organizational behavior management (OBM) consultation to organizations. They also note that they have several personnel and supervisors on staff who are "Certified in Applied Behavior Analysis." Carlos was offered the position. He was told that though they do not currently have any BCBAs on staff, they are looking to "expand their practice" and want Carlos to help build their ABA services.

Applicable Ethics Code(s):				
Rationale for Chosen Code(s):				
Code Violation?	Yes	No	Need More Information	If Situation Continues
Antecedent Factors Contributing to Scenario:				
Preventative Strategies:				
Ethical Course of Action:				
Future Risk Factors to Keep in Mind:				
Discussion Questions:				
What suggestions might you have if Carlos were to accept the position with the company?				

CASE 9: ACTING ETHICALLY

Committed ACTion Behavior Analysis provides ABA services primarily for individuals diagnosed with ASD. Many of the intervention plans for learners working with the agency incorporate Acceptance and Commitment Training (ACTraining). Gianna, a BCBA, was recently hired by Committed ACTion. She has been working as a behavior analyst for many years and has gained a lot of experience within the field. While she is very eager and excited to learn more about ACTraining, she has not yet had the opportunity within her professional experience to supervise intervention programs that include ACTraining elements. In reviewing her preliminary caseload, Gianna noticed that at least two of the learners she will be working with will be transferred from other BCBAs at Committed ACTion who have intervention plans that include ACTraining targets and goals.

Applicable Ethics Code(s):				
Rationale for Chosen Code(s):				
Code Violation?	Yes	No	Need More Information	If Situation Continues
Antecedent Factors Contributing to Scenario:				
Preventative Strategies:				
Ethical Course of Action:				
Future Risk Factors to Keep in Mind:				

CASE 10: IS THERE A DOCTOR IN THE HOUSE?

Devi, a 16-year-old diagnosed with ASD, was prescribed a medication by her primary care physician. Devi's parents are concerned with the medication's side effects, which include weight gain and lethargy. They plan to meet with the physician to discuss their apprehension, but first ask Elois, the BCBA supervising Devi's ABA services, her opinion on the continued use of the medication. Elois told Devi's parents that she is also disturbed by the side effects and does not feel the medication has been helpful. Elois recommends that the medication be discontinued.

Applicable Ethics Code(s):				
Rationale for Chosen Code(s):				
Code Violation?	Yes	No	Need More Information	If Situation Continues
Antecedent Factors Contributing to Scenario:				
Preventative Strategies:				
Ethical Course of Action:				
Future Risk Factors to Keep in Mind:				
Discussion Questions:				
How might your opinion of the scenario change if Elois included specific data related to Devi's behaviors since starting the medication with her recommendation to discontinue the medication?				

CASE 11: HOW DIFFERENT CAN IT BE?

Cameron is a BCBA working for an ABA agency. His state implemented mandatory lockdowns due to a current health crisis. While Cameron has several years of experience supervising face-to-face ABA services, he has never conducted intervention via telehealth. He is concerned that without continued ABA services, several of the learners on his caseload will demonstrate regression. Despite his lack of experience, he decides to transition all the learners on his caseload to receive telehealth services.

Applicable Ethics Code(s):				
Rationale for Chosen Code(s):				
Code Violation?	Yes	No	Need More Information	If Situation Continues
Antecedent Factors Contributing to Scenario:				
Preventative Strategies:				
Ethical Course of Action:				
Future Risk Factors to Keep in Mind:				
Discussion Questions:				
What considerations would you suggest Cameron make if instead of continuing services, he determined some of his learners would need to pause or discontinue services?				

CASE 12: REQUESTED REMOVAL

Reggie is a BCBA who was recently assigned a new learner, Alex, through his ABA agency for home-based intervention services. On his first day at Alex's home, Reggie discovers that Alex's parents are both men. Reggie is not comfortable within the home, so he asks to be removed from the case and to have one of the agency's other BCBAs take over supervisory responsibilities.

Applicable Ethics Code(s):				
Rationale for Chosen Code(s):				
Code Violation?	Yes	No	Need More Information	If Situation Continues
Antecedent Factors Contributing to Scenario:				
Preventative Strategies:				
Ethical Course of Action:				
Future Risk Factors to Keep in Mind:				

Discussion Questions:

How might your thoughts change if Reggie's agency did not have any other BCBAs available to take over supervisory responsibilities?

Given Reggie's discomfort working within the family's home, do you believe an ethical violation has occurred by his request to be removed from the case?

What, if any ethical responsibility might Reggie's BCBA supervisor have if the agency decided for Reggie to to continue to work with the family, and the Alex's fathers reported that they were disturbed when Alex came them and said Reggie told Alex that he personally believes a marriage should only be between a man and a woman?

CASE 13: HUMAN RESOURCES

Kendi and Sara provide job training and on-site support for the same adult learner. One of their responsibilities is to interact with the learner's boss and coworkers to help facilitate the learner's productivity and participation. While working with the learner, both have experienced and observed repeated sexist, racist, and ableist comments made by the learner's boss toward them and the learner. Kendi and Sara have reported these comments and their concern to the BCBA supervisor, who stated that the learner is working "within a different type of environment" and they will have to become accustomed to these types of comments.

Applicable Ethics Code(s):				
Rationale for Chosen Code(s):				
Code Violation?	Yes	No	Need More Information	If Situation Continues
Antecedent Factors Contributing to Scenario:				
Preventative Strategies:				
Ethical Course of Action:				
Future Risk Factors to Keep in Mind:				
Discussion Questions:				
Upon hearing the statements of Kendi and Sara, how would you suggest their BCBA supervisor respond?				

CASE 14: DISCRIMINATION DISCREPANCY

Every quarter, Jonie, a BCBA-D and Clinic Director at an ABA agency, conducts audits of the cases and super-vision allotments of the BCBAs within her company. She uses the data as an opportunity to assess overall out-comes, make more specific recommendations for the learners being served by the agency, review the supervisory practices of the BCBAs, and develop future trainings. After examining the caseload of Landon, one of the BCBAs at the agency, Jonie noticed a significant discrepancy in the number of parent-training hours provided to the lower-income families when compared with those from high socioeconomic statuses. In their discussion meeting to clarify the discrepancy, Landon stated, "It just seems like a waste of time to offer these people parent training when they are either always working, just sitting around or not interested."

Applicable Ethics Code(s):				
Rationale for Chosen Code(s):				
Code Violation?	Yes	No	Need More Information	If Situation Continues
Antecedent Factors Contributing to Scenario:				
Preventative Strategies:				
Ethical Course of Action:				
Future Risk Factors to Keep in Mind:				
Discussion Questions:				
Would the same ethics codes apply if, instead of Landon's assumptions and statement regarding the families, he had records documenting his repeated attempts to engage with the families that were receiving less training and developed a plan to address the barriers?				

CASE 15: EQUAL OPPORTUNITY

Possibilities ABA Agency recently accepted a new learner for home-based sessions. Nisha, a BCBA, has been assigned supervisory responsibilities. In reviewing the details of the case, Nisha learns that the family indicated their religion as a strong factor in their lives. They asked that any staff members who join their child's team consider faith-based integration within their practice or be considerate of the family's beliefs. The family has also endorsed a preference for male staff members but noted if female staff are included on the team, asked that they wear modest clothing that covers their shoulders when entering the family's home. Nisha identifies that, because of the religious preferences of the family, she does not feel comfortable providing supervision. She considers telling her employer that she will not work with the new learner but instead decides that she will keep the family on her caseload. She plans to conduct all supervision through remote platforms and by gathering feedback from the direct staff members rather than conducting in-person observations.

Applicable Ethics Code(s):				
Rationale for Chosen Code(s):				
Code Violation?	Yes	No	Need More Information	If Situation Continues
Antecedent Factors Contributing to Scenario:				
Preventative Strategies:				
Ethical Course of Action:				
Future Risk Factors to Keep in Mind:				
Discussion Questions:				
Would the same ethics codes apply if Nisha had stepped down from supervising the new learner and found an immediate replacement?				

CASE 16: CULTURAL CONCLUSIONS

Amy is an RBT who is accruing experience toward her BACB exam under the supervision of Sharon, a BCBA. Amy identifies as Asian-American. Sharon received a new learner on her caseload whose family recently immigrated from China. Since Amy and the new learner's family are of Asian descent, Sharon believes Amy would culturally be a good fit and a helpful addition to the learner's team. To join the new team, Amy will have to adjust her schedule and, as a result, will experience a reduction in the direct intervention she provides. The change will decrease her hourly paycheck, as well as her accrued experience hours toward sitting for the BACB exam.

Applicable Ethics Code(s):				
Rationale for Chosen Code(s):				
Code Violation?	Yes	No	Need More Information	If Situation Continues
Antecedent Factors Contributing to Scenario:				
Preventative Strategies:				
Ethical Course of Action:				
Future Risk Factors to Keep in Mind:				

CASE 17: CANCELED CONSIDERATIONS

Sheriece is a BCBA who has inherited several cases from another BCBA, Evelyn, who recently left their ABA agency. When Sheriece began working with the new cases, she discovered that one family's primary spoken language was Mandarin. Evelyn had not included a translator at any point during service provision, including during intake and goal setting. Instead, Evelyn relied on the learner's 7-year-old sister to do translations. Additionally, Evelyn set a goal for the learner to use a fork and spoon when eating when it was noted the parents had asked to teach the learner to use chopsticks first. There was a second case where Evelyn set a goal for a Black learner to wash her hair daily, even though the parents stated they wanted their daughter to wash her hair once per week. Sheriece noted an additional case that involved a family who were Jehovah's Witnesses. The family requested that curriculum targets not include information having to do with holidays such as birthdays, Christmas, and Easter since they are not celebrated. Evelyn followed through with avoiding targets related to Christmas and Easter, but she had the learner make a birthday card for the mother on her birthday.

Applicable Ethics Code(s):			
Rationale for Chosen Code(s):			
Code Violation?	Yes	No	Need More Information	If Situation Continues
Antecedent Factors Contributing to Scenario:			
Preventative Strategies:			
Ethical Course of Action:			
Future Risk Factors to Keep in Mind:			

CASE 18: BREAK UP, BREAK DOWN

Kai is a BCBA who is involved in a very tumultuous and difficult divorce. For the last several months, there has been a noticeable change in Kai's appearance and behavior. He stopped shaving (growing a scruffy and unruly beard) and is often noticed wearing the same, unwashed clothes several days in a row. Kai has also been observed on multiple occasions each week to arrive late for clinical team meetings, call out of work with little to no notice, lose track of conversations during parent trainings and calls, and yell at staff members in front of learners.

Applicable Ethics Code(s):				
Rationale for Chosen Code(s):				
Code Violation?	Yes	No	Need More Information	If Situation Continues
Antecedent Factors Contributing to Scenario:				
Preventative Strategies:				
Ethical Course of Action:				
Future Risk Factors to Keep in Mind:				
Discussion Questions:				
Would Kai's responsibility be different if he worked at a company with other BCBAs on staff or if he worked within his own independent practice?				
What might be the responsibilities of Kai's colleagues if he worked at a company with other BCBAs?				

CASE 19: REQUEST FOR SERVICE

Janie is a BCBA who owns and operates a small ABA agency (four other BCBAs on staff, along with additional administrative personnel) in a rural area. Marie, a woman who works in the agency's scheduling department, mentioned that her 2.5-year-old son received a diagnosis of ASD, and she is looking for available resources. Because Marie works in scheduling, she is very familiar with the clinical knowledge of the agency's BCBAs and is impressed by their level of training and the dedication of the staff. She has reviewed the agency's staffing and supervisory commitments and knows that they have the availability to take additional cases. She is also a member of one of the agency's accepted insurance carriers. Marie asks Janie if her son can participate in an intake assessment and receive services.

Applicable Ethics Code(s):				
Rationale for Chosen Code(s):				
Code Violation?	Yes	No	Need More Information	If Situation Continues
Antecedent Factors Contributing to Scenario:				
Preventative Strategies:				
Ethical Course of Action:				
Future Risk Factors to Keep in Mind:				
Discussion Questions:				
What are some ethical challenges that could arise should Janie accept Marie's son as a client? What are the issues that she might address if she does not accept Marie's son as a client?				

CASE 20: UNFRIEND REQUEST

Victoria is a BCBA working primarily within the home setting. One day after work, she noticed a "friend request" on one of her personal social media accounts from the father of one of the learners on her caseload. She did not respond to the request before her session the next day, during which the learner's father asked Victoria if she received his request and why she had not responded. He mentioned that he has a right to know about the people who come into his home and work with his son.

Applicable Ethics Code(s):				
Rationale for Chosen Code(s):				
Code Violation?	Yes	No	Need More Information	If Situation Continues
Antecedent Factors Contributing to Scenario:				
Preventative Strategies:				
Ethical Course of Action:				
Future Risk Factors to Keep in Mind:				
Discussion Questions:				
Would Victoria's response to the situation, or her ethical responsibility be different, if her social media profile was public versus private?				

CASE 21: PARTY TIME

Solomon is an 18-year-old man who receives two, individual-based, 3-hour social skills training and support sessions a week with Jasmine, a BCBA. In 2 weeks, Solomon's parents are hosting a graduation party for Solomon over the weekend and have asked Jasmine to attend. Solomon's parents have suggested they reschedule one of Jasmine's regular sessions that would have been held during the week and use the service hours during the graduation party.

Applicable Ethics Code(s):				
Rationale for Chosen Code(s):				
Code Violation?	Yes	No	Need More Information	If Situation Continues
Antecedent Factors Contributing to Scenario:				
Preventative Strategies:				
Ethical Course of Action:				
Future Risk Factors to Keep in Mind:				
Discussion Questions:				
Under what conditions would you consider Jasmine's attendance at Solomon's graduation party ethically appropriate?				
Under what conditions might her attendance be ethically problematic?				

CASE 22: THE ONLY ONE FOR THE JOB

Mahalia has lived all of her life in a small rural town that is more than 200 miles from the nearest mid-sized city. She is a BCBA working in a school district and has specific training in assessing and treating severe challenging behavior. Her best friend is Alma, has been the Special Education Coordinator in the district, was just promoted to the position of Director of Special Education. With her promotion, Alma is now Mahalia's direct supervisor. Alma's son is in kindergarten and receives special education services. Recently, he has begun to engage in severe aggression, and his IEP team has initiated a request for a Functional Behavior Assessment (FBA). Mahalia is the only person in the district who is qualified to lead the team in conducting the FBA.

Applicable Ethics Code(s):				
Rationale for Chosen Code(s):				
Code Violation?	Yes	No	Need More Information	If Situation Continues
Antecedent Factors Contributing to Scenario:				
Preventative Strategies:				
Ethical Course of Action:				
Future Risk Factors to Keep in Mind:				
Discussion Questions:				
What might be the ethical challenges if Mahalia were to conduct the FBA with Alma's son?				
What challenges could arise if Mahalia were to decline to conduct the assessment with Alma's son?				

CASE 23: SOMEONE'S GOTTA DO IT

Katie and Janet are BCBAs at a small clinic where they supervise ABA services for children d[...] and related disorders. Each BCBA has a caseload of eight learners. The clinic is in a small, [...] next closest ABA agency over 100 miles away. Katie's daughter is in the same middle sch[...] sister of one of Janet's cases (Tommy). The girls are close friends and frequently spend tim[...] school, hanging out at each other's houses, having sleepovers, and attending family dinn[...] friendship, the families frequently spend time with each other at community events and at [...] Due to a serious illness in the family, Janet needs to immediately move to another state, and Katie takes over all of Janet's cases (including Tommy) until another BCBA can be hired, which will likely take at least several months.

Applicable Ethics Code(s):				
Rationale for Chosen Code(s):				
Code Violation?	Yes	No	Need More Information	If Situation Continues
Antecedent Factors Contributing to Scenario:				
Preventative Strategies:				
Ethical Course of Action:				
Future Risk Factors to Keep in Mind:				
Discussion Questions:				
What precautions would you suggest Katie take if she were to accept the supervisory responsibilities of Tommy's case?				

CASE 24: I KNOW THAT GUY

Juan is an RBT at an agency providing residential services for adults with intellectual disabilities and is accruing supervised experience hours toward his BCBA with Dan, a BCBA at the same agency. Juan signs his daughter up for the local youth soccer team. At the first meeting, Juan finds out that Dan is the soccer coach for the team.

Applicable Ethics Code(s):				
Rationale for Chosen Code(s):				
Code Violation?	Yes	No	Need More Information	If Situation Continues
Antecedent Factors Contributing to Scenario:				
Preventative Strategies:				
Ethical Course of Action:				
Future Risk Factors to Keep in Mind:				

CASE 25: LACK OF SNACK

Riya is an RBT working in the home setting. She has been working with the same learner, Shaan, for a little over 1 year and has established a positive rapport with the learner and his family. The majority of Riya's sessions occur immediately after Shaan comes home from school. Riya notices that Shaan is often hungry and tired at the start of the session. Even though he eventually participates, his performance is significantly improved after having a snack. Riya has asked Shaan's parents to have a snack ready either at the start of, or prior to her session. However, on most occasions, there is no food in the house that Shaan will eat. During one of her sessions, Riya overheard Shaan's parents discussing their financial concerns and mentioning that they are not sure if they will have enough money to afford their rent and bills. Riya has started bringing her own food to the sessions to provide to Shaan.

Applicable Ethics Code(s):				
Rationale for Chosen Code(s):				
Code Violation?	Yes	No	Need More Information	If Situation Continues
Antecedent Factors Contributing to Scenario:				
Preventative Strategies:				
Ethical Course of Action:				
Future Risk Factors to Keep in Mind:				
Discussion Questions:				
How would you suggest Riya's BCBA supervisor assist with this situation?				

CASE 26: ETHICAL HEADACHE

Kona is a BCBA providing supervision at a learner's home. In the morning, Kona had a slight headache, and as the day continued, his headache progressed. When Kona arrived at the learner's house, his head was pounding. The learner's parents noticed Kona rubbing his temples and offered a bottle of water and a few aspirin.

Applicable Ethics Code(s):				
Rationale for Chosen Code(s):				
Code Violation?	Yes	No	Need More Information	If Situation Continues
Antecedent Factors Contributing to Scenario:				
Preventative Strategies:				
Ethical Course of Action:				
Future Risk Factors to Keep in Mind:				
Discussion Questions:				
Are there any ethical implications to which Kona should be aware if he had cancelled his session because of his headache?				

CASE 27: SHARING IS CARING

Every 2 weeks, Carmen, a BCBA, meets the parents of a learner, whose program she supervises in the family home, for parent training and program review. At each meeting, the parents have placed some type of food or snack on the table for everyone to share. Carmen has politely declined the offer on each occasion. While at the office, a staff member who conducts sessions with the learner informed Carmen that the parents mentioned they are upset and slightly insulted that they have gone through the trouble of making food for their meetings with Carmen, and she never accepts. Not wanting to offend the parents, at their next meeting, Carmen thanks the parents for providing food and tells them that she is on a diet. The parents thank Carmen for addressing the issue. At the next parent training meeting, Carmen arrives to find a large vegetable plate and fruit salads for her and the parents to share. The parents say they want to be supportive of Carmen's diet and thank her for the services she provides to their daughter.

Applicable Ethics Code(s):				
Rationale for Chosen Code(s):				
Code Violation?	Yes	No	Need More Information	If Situation Continues
Antecedent Factors Contributing to Scenario:				
Preventative Strategies:				
Ethical Course of Action:				
Future Risk Factors to Keep in Mind:				
Discussion Questions:				
What might Carmen need to be aware of if she accepts the offer of the fruits and vegetables? What might she have to be aware of if she declines?				
How might Carmen be considerate of the family's cultural background in responding to the offer of food?				

CASE 28: SEASON PASS

Ethan is a BCBA who provides direct behavioral intervention to Kevin, a 10-year-old boy diagnosed with ASD. Kevin's family lives very close to a large amusement park and enjoys taking family trips to the park several times a year. Kevin's parents have expressed a desire to bring Kevin to the park more often to bond as a family. However, Kevin often struggles with the large crowds, waiting in line, and remaining within a safe proximity to the family. The parents have asked Ethan to join the family at the amusement park during select sessions to practice skills and increase safe behaviors. Since Ethan will likely join the family at the park across several occasions, Kevin's parents have offered to cover the cost of Ethan's tickets. Kevin's parents noted it would be less expensive to purchase Ethan a season pass. Since the pass will be in Ethan's name, it can be used during visits with Kevin and his family, as well as any other times Ethan may wish to enter the park on his own.

Applicable Ethics Code(s):				
Rationale for Chosen Code(s):				
Code Violation?	Yes	No	Need More Information	If Situation Continues
Antecedent Factors Contributing to Scenario:				
Preventative Strategies:				
Ethical Course of Action:				
Future Risk Factors to Keep in Mind:				
Discussion Questions:				
Would the same ethics code(s) apply if Ethan agreed to only use the season pass to the amusement park when visiting with Kevin's family?				
Would the same ethics code(s) apply if Ethan purchased the amusement park tickets using his own money?				

CASE 29: MORE THAN FRIENDS

Abigail is an RBT receiving supervised experience hours from Jeremiah, a BCBA. The two have worked together for almost a year and have developed a positive rapport. After work, Jeremiah asks Abigail if she would like to go out with him on a date for dinner and some drinks.

Applicable Ethics Code(s):				
Rationale for Chosen Code(s):				
Code Violation?	Yes	No	Need More Information	If Situation Continues
Antecedent Factors Contributing to Scenario:				
Preventative Strategies:				
Ethical Course of Action:				
Future Risk Factors to Keep in Mind:				
Discussion Questions:				
Would the ethical implications be different if Abigail asked Jeremiah out to dinner?				

CASE 30: SWIPE LEFT

Tobias, a BCBA, is a member of a dating app community. He received a message that he matched with Victor, who is a member of the training cohort Tobias supervises for those studying and accruing hours to sit for the BACB exam. Victor messaged Tobias through the app and said that he plans to take his exam this weekend and would like to get together to celebrate after he passes.

Applicable Ethics Code(s):				
Rationale for Chosen Code(s):				
Code Violation?	Yes	No	Need More Information	If Situation Continues
Antecedent Factors Contributing to Scenario:				
Preventative Strategies:				
Ethical Course of Action:				
Future Risk Factors to Keep in Mind:				
Discussion Questions:				
Would Tobias or Victor's ethical obligations be different if Victor reached out to Tobias before he scheduled his exam? What if he reached out after he officially learned he passed?				

CASE 31: JUST NOT INTO YOU

While hanging out at a bar with some friends, Imelda, a BCBA, was approached by Matthias, the father of a learner who "graduated" from ABA services with Imelda approximately 1 year ago. The two briefly catch up and discuss Matthias' son's current progress. Before parting ways, the two confirmed they both still had the same contact information. The next day, Imelda received a text message from Matthias asking if she would be interested in meeting for a date.

Applicable Ethics Code(s):				
Rationale for Chosen Code(s):				
Code Violation?	Yes	No	Need More Information	If Situation Continues
Antecedent Factors Contributing to Scenario:				
Preventative Strategies:				
Ethical Course of Action:				
Future Risk Factors to Keep in Mind:				
Discussion Questions:				
Do you believe there are any changes in Imelda's ethical responsibilities if Matthias is currently married to his son's other parent?				

CASE 32: OLD FLAME

Nasir and Winona work for the same ABA agency. The two dated for about 2 years but called things off about 4 months ago. Since that time, Nasir has started to pursue his BACB coursework and certification. Winona is the only BCBA working at the company with immediate availability to begin providing Nasir with BCBA supervision.

Applicable Ethics Code(s):				
Rationale for Chosen Code(s):				
Code Violation?	Yes	No	Need More Information	If Situation Continues
Antecedent Factors Contributing to Scenario:				
Preventative Strategies:				
Ethical Course of Action:				
Future Risk Factors to Keep in Mind:				
Discussion Questions:				
Do you believe the same ethics code(s) would apply if Nasir and Winona had been dating for less time?				

CASE 33: SLIPPED MY MIND

Ella, a BCBA, has been asked by the parents of Gordon, a learner she works with, for a copy of the most recent progress report. Gordon's parents would like to bring the report with them to his upcoming doctor's appointment. Though the report is complete and all the information is available, Ella did not bring the report with her when she attended Gordon's session for an observation. Gordon's parents reminded Ella again of the doctor's appointment and requested that she send them the document as soon as possible. Ella's company does have access to an encrypted and secure email system. However, Ella did not email or deliver the report before the scheduled doctor's appointment.

Applicable Ethics Code(s):				
Rationale for Chosen Code(s):				
Code Violation?	Yes	No	Need More Information	If Situation Continues
Antecedent Factors Contributing to Scenario:				
Preventative Strategies:				
Ethical Course of Action:				
Future Risk Factors to Keep in Mind:				
Discussion Questions:				
How might you suggest Ella approach the request by Gordon's parents if she had concerns with how the information included within the progress report would be understood or interpreted?				

Charise is a BCBA who oversees ABA services for a learner within the school setting. As part of her agency's contract with the school, all staff working in the classroom have undergone criminal background checks. One of the RBTs, who typically works with the learner, had to take an approved and planned leave of absence. Charise replaced the absent staff member with another RBT who works within her agency. However, since this replacement does not typically work in the same school, they have not completed the expected background check.

Applicable Ethics Code(s):				
Rationale for Chosen Code(s):				
Code Violation?	Yes	No	Need More Information	If Situation Continues
Antecedent Factors Contributing to Scenario:				
Preventative Strategies:				
Ethical Course of Action:				
Future Risk Factors to Keep in Mind:				
Discussion Questions:				
What might be the clinical and ethical implications if, instead of adding the staff member who did not have a background check, Charise's agency did not fulfill the intervention hours typically performed by the absent RBT?				

CASE 35: UNDER THE INFLUENCE

A few months ago, an ABA agency held their annual BCBA party, where alcohol was served. A few of the staff drank heavily, including Nitya, a newly certified BCBA. Nitya was pulled over by the police on the way home, arrested, and charged with driving under the influence (DUI). As part of her guilty plea, she had to pay a fine, participate in community service, and complete a DUI education class. When asked by her colleagues if she reported anything to the BACB about the incident, Nitya stated that she did not. She said she felt it was already embarrassing enough, and because she told her agency about the DUI, she did not have to inform the BACB about something that happened out of the office.

Applicable Ethics Code(s):				
Rationale for Chosen Code(s):				
Code Violation?	Yes	No	Need More Information	If Situation Continues
Antecedent Factors Contributing to Scenario:				
Preventative Strategies:				
Ethical Course of Action:				
Future Risk Factors to Keep in Mind:				
Discussion Questions:				
Would Nitya's response to her arrest and charges be different if she had not attended a work function with fellow BCBAs?				
Do you believe the agency where Nitya works holds any responsibility related to Nitya's level of intoxication and arrest?				

CASE 36: IT'S JUST BUSINESS

Blythe is a BCBA-D who owns a small ABA agency and is interested in growing her practice. She has offered an opportunity for the BCBAs she currently has on staff to participate in potential client outreach, wherein the BCBAs will be given bonuses dependent on the number of new clients they bring into the agency.

Applicable Ethics Code(s):				
Rationale for Chosen Code(s):				
Code Violation?	Yes	No	Need More Information	If Situation Continues
Antecedent Factors Contributing to Scenario:				
Preventative Strategies:				
Ethical Course of Action:				
Future Risk Factors to Keep in Mind:				

CASE 37: GENTLE NUDGE

Stephanie, a BCBA and owner of an ABA agency, is housemates with Amara, an RBT who works for Stephanie's company. Amara is accumulating supervision hours toward her BCBA credential with Rudy, another BCBA who works within Stephanie's agency. All staff members who are receiving supervision at Stephanie's company participate in regular performance evaluations based on the BACB's Task List. Stephanie approached Rudy after Amara's most recent review and asked why Amara's performance score was lower than expected and encouraged Rudy to "take another look" and "work harder to support his supervisees."

Applicable Ethics Code(s):				
Rationale for Chosen Code(s):				
Code Violation?	Yes	No	Need More Information	If Situation Continues
Antecedent Factors Contributing to Scenario:				
Preventative Strategies:				
Ethical Course of Action:				
Future Risk Factors to Keep in Mind:				
Discussion Questions:				
What might be the ethical challenges if Rudy were to "reevaluate" Amara's performance?				
Has Stephanie absolved her ethical responsibilities since she is not directly responsible for the supervision of Amara, her friend and housemate?				

Chapter 6

Section 2: Responsibility in Practice

From the beginning stages of our field, it became clear that behavior could be influenced through the implementation of strategies and procedures previously employed and developed within more traditional laboratory settings. However, it was not yet clear in whose best interest these behavior changes were to occur. In many cases, the focus was placed on the interest of the employers of the behavior analysts. That is, the "client" was not necessarily the individual being directly impacted by the goals of intervention. Instead, goals were focused on the needs of the group or institution that hired the behavior analyst. Thus, while the challenging behavior of such learners may have been reduced, these behavior changes were facilitated to better serve the environment within which the learner resided, rather than for the increased autonomy, independence, or quality of life of the learner (Bailey & Burch, 2016).

Though behavior analysts had the ability to manipulate the environments to serve the interests of institutions, it became more apparent that without the individual's best interest as the paramount focus, effective intervention could also be harmful and abusive. From this change in perspective, there was a structural shift in which behavior analytic strategies were applied, with the most vulnerable individual identified as the primary client and direct focal point of service. By dedicating clinical efforts toward the individual who was least able to advocate for themselves, behavior analysts were able to institute meaningful change not only in the life of the person but also for those collaterally involved (Leaf et al., 2021).

Section 2 of the Behavior Analyst Certification Board (BACB) Ethics Code (2020b) emphasizes the practices and procedures behavior analysts may take in best assuring the interests of learners are of highest priority and that appropriate stakeholders are involved and invested throughout the process to inform beneficial decision-making and intervention strategies. To facilitate a responsible practice that includes learners and those immediately affected by behavior-analytic intervention, independent data related to the behavior in question must be collected. Much of the information received by behavior analysts is based on anecdotal accounts from those who have direct interaction with learners. For example, parents may report a concern related to a particularly challenging behavior, teachers may describe a skill deficit that is interfering with a student's learning, and employers may note issues related to overall workflow and productivity. While this information is extremely important and should not be dismissed, a behavior analyst must not rely solely on these subjective statements when determining areas of need and when developing intervention plans. Without observing the target behavior and related corresponding variables, a behavior analyst may inadvertently implement intervention strategies that are inappropriate, ineffective, and/or unnecessary (Tarbox et al., 2011).

A Workbook of Ethical Case Scenarios in Applied Behavior Analysis, Second Edition. https://doi.org/10.1016/B978-0-323-98813-1.00006-2

An aspect that distinguishes applied behavior analysis (ABA) from other related fields is its reliance on data collection to make informed decisions regarding behavioral strategies and interventions. Assessing behavior involves record review, indirect assessment through interviews and questionnaires, and direct assessment via observation, including the collection of baseline data to demonstrate preintervention levels of the target behavior. Additionally, once an intervention is in place, ongoing assessment occurs through continued data collection that depicts the effects of the intervention (Tarbox et al., 2011). By conducting a comprehensive assessment prior to and during implementation, behavior analysts are better able to take responsibility in accounting for any behavior change that may result from the intervention.

As not all individuals involved with the behavior-analytic intervention will have the time or skill set to evaluate the information gathered, it becomes increasingly important for behavior analysts to explain and discuss assessment findings in a manner that is easily understandable and meaningful. Even the most well-researched and thorough interventions can fail before they begin if those directly involved in the intervention lack understanding of their direction, purpose, or practice. Furthermore, in order to ensure practices are socially valid, it is essential to take a collaborative approach with clients when identifying intervention goals and developing intervention plans. The voices, preferences, and wishes of those that will be served must be heard and addressed in order to actualize an intervention approach that demonstrates compassionate care (Taylor et al., 2019), does no harm, and demonstrates cultural humility.

Perhaps one of the more controversial aspects of interventions based in ABA is the use and implementation of restrictive or punishment-based procedures. Such strategies focus on the elimination or reduction of a specified behavior through the presentation or removal of a particular stimulus. In many cases, the presented stimulus may be considered aversive to the individual who engages in the targeted behavior identified for reduction. Likewise, the stimulus removed is likely one that is valued or preferred by the individual. Punishment-based strategies are often effective in quickly eliminating targeted behaviors, and when consistently implemented, have the potential of maintaining the reduction (Cooper et al., 2020).

Unfortunately, punishment can be reinforcing for the individual implementing the punishment-based procedure, resulting in the use of punishment strategies instead of reinforcement-based procedures that focus on the development of adaptive and appropriate replacement behavior and skills. As these strategies become more inherent, the individual implementing the punishment-based procedure may increase the frequency or intensity of the punishment as a means of maintaining the behavior change. Similarly, the use of punishment-based procedures may generalize across other behaviors viewed as requiring reduction. Utilizing punishment-based procedures may also continue to be reinforced as their implementation may result in a reduction of stress and increase in satisfaction as the individual employing the punishment-based strategy experiences a sense of personal responsibility for affecting the behavior change and an assumption that they have taken active control of the challenging situation (Dawson, 2004).

Behavior analysts have learned that behavior can be effectively altered through reliance on reinforcement strategies. Yet, both the appeal and risk of including punishment procedures are important to acknowledge and address. Doing so suggests the use of punishment strategies only when absolutely clinically necessary and requires the behavior analyst to actively reflect on their rationale for including punishment procedures within behavior-change programs prior to implementation. As such, it is explicitly noted within Section 2 of the Code that reinforcement procedures are used and recommended whenever possible, and any inclusion of punishment interventions are only incorporated following the use of reinforcement strategies as an adjunctive strategy with reinforcement procedures when (1) desired results have not been obtained through less intrusive means; (2) the risk of harm to the learner is more prominent than the risk of implementing the punishment-based strategy; (3) required review processes have been followed; (4) data collection and observation is conducted to ensure appropriate implementation, effectiveness, and necessity of the strategy; and (5) the punishment-based procedure is modified or discontinued when no longer necessary or has been determined to be ineffective (BACB, 2020b).

CASE 38: NO "I" IN TEAM

Anvi is the Board Certified Behavior Analyst (BCBA) representative on a multidisciplinary Individualized Education Plan (IEP) team. At each IEP meeting, one of the other professionals consistently recommends strategies that are not supported by research. Though Anvi advocates for evidence-based interventions, the rest of the IEP team is considering including one of the nonevidence-based suggestions within the student's IEP, which would require Anvi's staff to be responsible for implementing and collecting data on the intervention.

Applicable Ethics Code(s):				
Rationale for Chosen Code(s):				
Code Violation?	Yes	No	Need More Information	If Situation Continues
Antecedent Factors Contributing to Scenario:				
Preventative Strategies:				
Ethical Course of Action:				
Future Risk Factors to Keep in Mind:				
Discussion Questions:				
What would you do if the IEP team showed you two single-subject research design studies demonstrating that the intervention they are considering has been effective?				
Would your consideration of the nonevidence-based intervention change if the rest of the IEP team agreed to discontinue the nonevidence-based treatment should your data reveal that it is ineffective?				

CASE 39: WALKING BILLBOARD

Advanced Autism Services is a nonpublic agency, providing ABA services for children, teens, and adults diagnosed with Autism Spectrum Disorder (ASD) and other developmental disabilities (DDs) within the clinic, home, school, and community settings. When providing clinic-based services, staff members are asked by management to wear an agency uniform (either a collared shirt or agency t-shirt) that has the agency's logo prominently displayed on the front. Staff are told that the uniform helps to ensure that staff are dressed appropriately and professionally in clothing that allows them to address any clinical need or manage challenging behavior, as well as helping the learners identify who they may access for assistance. Many of the staff provide services to individuals completely within the clinic setting; however, others provide services to several individuals in different locations depending on the learner and the time of day. Out of convenience, many staff remain within their agency uniform as they provide services to learners outside of the clinic setting, such as in the community or within schools.

Applicable Ethics Code(s):				
Rationale for Chosen Code(s):				
Code Violation?	Yes	No	Need More Information	If Situation Continues
Antecedent Factors Contributing to Scenario:				
Preventative Strategies:				
Ethical Course of Action:				
Future Risk Factors to Keep in Mind:				
Discussion Questions:				
Would your thoughts related to applicable ethics codes, or your suggested responses to the scenario change, if the agency's name was "Advanced Services" instead of "Advanced Autism Services?"				

CASE 40: WORD OF MOUTH

Carlos, a BCBA, is conducting an observation of a learner named Chase in the school setting when approached by the parent of another student in Chase's class. The parent told Carlos that she is interested in starting ABA services for her daughter and has been looking for an agency. She mentioned that the teacher told her to speak with Carlos since he is a BCBA supervising Chase's program. She asked for Carlos's business card so she could speak to him about initiating services with his agency.

Applicable Ethics Code(s):				
Rationale for Chosen Code(s):				
Code Violation?	Yes	No	Need More Information	If Situation Continues
Antecedent Factors Contributing to Scenario:				
Preventative Strategies:				
Ethical Course of Action:				
Future Risk Factors to Keep in Mind:				
Discussion Questions:				
What might be the ethical implications if Carlos provides the interested parent with his business card?				
Does Carlos have any ethical or clinical obligations to the new parent or student who is interested in his services?				

CASE 41: HOLIDAY SPIRIT

Over the holiday season, Asha, a BCBA-D and owner of Kids Konnect Behavioral Services, receives several holiday cards with pictures of the children and families to whom her company provides ABA services. As a demonstration of appreciation, Asha displays the cards in the waiting room of the front office on the "Kids Konnect Announcements" bulletin board.

Applicable Ethics Code(s):				
Rationale for Chosen Code(s):				
Code Violation?	Yes	No	Need More Information	If Situation Continues
Antecedent Factors Contributing to Scenario:				
Preventative Strategies:				
Ethical Course of Action:				
Future Risk Factors to Keep in Mind:				
Discussion Questions:				
Do you feel as though Asha's ethical responsibilities are different since the families sent the cards with pictures?				
How might Asha display or convey her appreciation to the families in a different way?				

CASE 42: COFFEE TALK

Hector is a BCBA supervising home-based services for Sonia. Hector typically conducts treatment team meetings and supervision for the direct staff members who work with Sonia within the family's home. However, due to changes in scheduling, home meetings are no longer an option. If meetings are held within Hector's office, one or more staff members will likely be unable to attend. Hector has found a coffee shop that is centrally located for all the staff and plans to hold meetings at this location, since everyone will be able to attend, until Sonia's parents are able to host meetings at their home again.

Applicable Ethics Code(s):				
Rationale for Chosen Code(s):				
Code Violation?	Yes	No	Need More Information	If Situation Continues
Antecedent Factors Contributing to Scenario:				
Preventative Strategies:				
Ethical Course of Action:				
Future Risk Factors to Keep in Mind:				
Discussion Questions:				
What suggestions might you have for Hector to ensure consistency and provide support if the staff members working with Sonia are unable to attend the regularly scheduled team meetings?				

CASE 43: DECORATION DILEMMA

Kira is a BCBA who is remodeling the office space at her ABA agency, as well as updating her company's website and social media pages. She wants to give the company a more personal feel by showcasing pictures of staff and learners across her internet platforms and within her office space. She asks the Registered Behavior Technicians (RBTs) to text her pictures of learners taken on their phones during their sessions.

Applicable Ethics Code(s):				
Rationale for Chosen Code(s):				
Code Violation?	Yes	No	Need More Information	If Situation Continues
Antecedent Factors Contributing to Scenario:				
Preventative Strategies:				
Ethical Course of Action:				
Future Risk Factors to Keep in Mind:				
Discussion Questions:				
What are your thoughts about RBTs taking photographs of the learners?				
What concerns might you have if RBTs use their phones during sessions with learners?				
What might be the ethical implications if Kira reached out to the learner's parents for a photographic release prior to showcasing the pictures throughout the office?				

CASE 44: SCAM LIKELY

Greg, a BCBA, receives a telephone call while at his office from Sally, who states that she works for the Student Services Department at the local university. Sally is calling to confirm John, a new student, receives ABA services from Greg so that she may enroll him in the university's available resource groups and collaborate with Greg about John's services. Greg has been supporting John in transitioning to his new school and has encouraged him to contact the university's programs but was not aware John had followed through with the recommendation.

Applicable Ethics Code(s):				
Rationale for Chosen Code(s):				
Code Violation?	Yes	No	Need More Information	If Situation Continues
Antecedent Factors Contributing to Scenario:				
Preventative Strategies:				
Ethical Course of Action:				
Future Risk Factors to Keep in Mind:				
Discussion Questions:				
If John had told Greg he reached out to the university's Student Services Department, would the applicable ethics codes or your advice to Greg change?				

CASE 45: MY PASSWORD IS "PASSWORD"

Sally, an RBT, had her car broken into while parked at a local coffee shop between clients. In addition to several personal items missing, Sally's company's tablet, which contained learner data, contact information, and programming details, was stolen from her front seat. The tablet requires a four-digit passcode to unlock the device and a personalized password to access learner records.

Applicable Ethics Code(s):				
Rationale for Chosen Code(s):				
Code Violation?	Yes	No	Need More Information	If Situation Continues
Antecedent Factors Contributing to Scenario:				
Preventative Strategies:				
Ethical Course of Action:				
Future Risk Factors to Keep in Mind:				
Discussion Questions:				
Would your thoughts regarding whether a violation had occurred change if, instead of a password protected tablet, the learner's records were kept in a paper binder?				

CASE 46: NEED A NAP

Trisha is a BCBA working at an ABA agency within the clinic setting. Most of the individuals she works with at the clinic are dropped off in the mornings and receive services continuously throughout the day, depending on their needs. Some of the learners Trisha supervises are young children who take naps. Trisha and her staff typically record when naps occur and when active instruction is taking place. This information is provided to the company's administrative department. After reviewing the funding authorization requests for several of the individuals on her caseload, Trisha noticed that her agency bills the entire day, including the times when the learners are napping, as active intervention.

Applicable Ethics Code(s):				
Rationale for Chosen Code(s):				
Code Violation?	Yes	No	Need More Information	If Situation Continues
Antecedent Factors Contributing to Scenario:				
Preventative Strategies:				
Ethical Course of Action:				
Future Risk Factors to Keep in Mind:				
Discussion Questions:				
Does the billing department have an ethical responsibility to their clients, the company, or the funding source in this scenario?				

CASE 47: BILLING BLUNDER

Tarik is a BCBA who works at a large ABA agency with multiple departments that provide various behavior-based services to individuals with DDs including ABA intervention, parent support groups, family therapy, and respite services. Tarik received an audit from the funding organization for one of the individuals on his caseload. In reviewing his documentation and the billing information submitted, Tarik noticed consistent weekly occurrences when his company billed for ABA services that were not provided to the learner. In researching the discrepancy, Tarik found that the company did provide respite services, which are not part of the family's authorized funding, during those times that were billed as intervention based in ABA. Tarik knows how much the family has benefited from the support and relief the respite services have provided.

Applicable Ethics Code(s):				
Rationale for Chosen Code(s):				
Code Violation?	Yes	No	Need More Information	If Situation Continues
Antecedent Factors Contributing to Scenario:				
Preventative Strategies:				
Ethical Course of Action:				
Future Risk Factors to Keep in Mind:				

CASE 48: HIDDEN FEES

Penny, a BCBA, is in the process of completing the introductory paperwork and intake process for a new learner. While confirming the family's insurance information and coverage, Penny noticed the family has a particularly high copayment responsibility. She is concerned this expectation may be a barrier for the family to participate in services. Penny is hopeful that her company will be able to work out an alternative option once services are initiated. Since the family did not specifically ask about copayments during the initial meetings, Penny decided not to mention the fee.

Applicable Ethics Code(s):				
Rationale for Chosen Code(s):				
Code Violation?	Yes	No	Need More Information	If Situation Continues
Antecedent Factors Contributing to Scenario:				
Preventative Strategies:				
Ethical Course of Action:				
Future Risk Factors to Keep in Mind:				

CASE 49: MONOLINGUAL MESS

Krissy, a BCBA, recently started working with Jasmin, a new learner. Jasmin and her family speak Spanish as the primary language within their home. The parents have expressed a preference for intervention to be conducted in Spanish, as they believe this will assist Jasmin in communicating and connecting with her family and will allow for family support and involvement in learning objectives. While Krissy does speak Spanish and is able to communicate effectively with Jasmin's family, she does not currently have any available RBTs who speak Spanish to join Jasmin's team. Given the lack of available Spanish-speaking staff and that Jasmin will be enrolled in an English-speaking school, Krissy informs the family that she and her team will be conducting all intervention programming in English.

Applicable Ethics Code(s):				
Rationale for Chosen Code(s):				
Code Violation?	Yes	No	Need More Information	If Situation Continues
Antecedent Factors Contributing to Scenario:				
Preventative Strategies:				
Ethical Course of Action:				
Future Risk Factors to Keep in Mind:				
Discussion Questions:				
What potential additional ethics code(s) might apply if Krissy insisted on services being conducted in English because she stated that anyone who lives in the United States should speak English?				

CASE 50: IDENTITY FIRST

Elton participates in ABA services with Janel, a BCBA. Although he has repeatedly told the members of his ABA team that he prefers to be referred to as "autistic" rather than a "person with autism," Janel and her team continue to introduce Elton using person-first language. Elton's behavior intervention plan includes "Stereotypical Behaviors" as a target for reduction. Elton has discussed with his team that he understands he may engage in some finger-pointing behavior, particularly when he is having difficulty with school assignments, but does not believe the behavior is an issue for concern. Elton's plan lists the behavior under the heading "Problem Behaviors" along with "Noncompliance" and "Vocal Protest."

Applicable Ethics Code(s):				
Rationale for Chosen Code(s):				
Code Violation?	Yes	No	Need More Information	If Situation Continues
Antecedent Factors Contributing to Scenario:				
Preventative Strategies:				
Ethical Course of Action:				
Future Risk Factors to Keep in Mind:				

CASE 51: SAFETY FIRST

Sonja is a BCBA providing consultative services for individuals who engage in severe or persistent dangerous behaviors within an adult inpatient hospital setting. She received a request to develop a behavior support plan to assist in the reduction of self-injurious head banging for an adult patient in the hospital. Based on the preliminary hospital staff report, head banging has increased significantly over the last 2 months. The hospital staff have attempted to stop the behavior when it occurs, but the patient is also very aggressive toward others, resulting in several staff injuries. The hospital staff have not yet attempted preventative strategies beyond offering the use of a padded helmet, which the patient refuses or promptly removes once placed. Hospital records indicate that the patient has a drainage shunt inserted in her head to assist with hydrocephalus. However, the patient has missed her last several appointments to assess the shunt due to aggressive behavior during transport to the medical professional.

Applicable Ethics Code(s):				
Rationale for Chosen Code(s):				
Code Violation?	Yes	No	Need More Information	If Situation Continues
Antecedent Factors Contributing to Scenario:				
Preventative Strategies:				
Ethical Course of Action:				
Future Risk Factors to Keep in Mind:				
Discussion Questions:				
Do you believe the same ethics code(s) would apply if the patient had attended their medical appointment to ensure the shunt was working properly?				

CASE 52: PREEMPTIVE PLAN

Antoine is a BCBA working within a residential facility for adults with developmental disabilities (DDs). One of his cases, Derek, has begun engaging in more frequent and severe episodes of aggressive behavior, resulting in several staff injuries and causing one other learner at the facility to require significant medical attention. Antoine has heard from the hospital staff that Derek rarely seeks out others to engage in aggression and only aggresses when others are near him. Antoine develops a behavior plan that focuses on the staff decreasing their direct contact with Derek and reducing expectations. The plan includes teaching strategies aimed at increasing Derek's appropriate requests to ask for breaks or to receive space and provides reactive strategies should Derek engage in aggression. The behavior plan also includes crisis management techniques to increase staff and peer safety in the event an aggressive incident occurs. After discussing and receiving approval for the plan by Derek and his guardians, Antoine trains staff and implements the plan within the residential setting.

Applicable Ethics Code(s):				
Rationale for Chosen Code(s):				
Code Violation?	Yes	No	Need More Information	If Situation Continues
Antecedent Factors Contributing to Scenario:				
Preventative Strategies:				
Ethical Course of Action:				
Future Risk Factors to Keep in Mind:				
Discussion Questions:				
Does Antoine's ethical responsibility to the Code change considering Derek's severe aggression?				
Would Antoine's responsibility be different if Derek engaged in less harmful behaviors?				
What are the concerns that could arise given Antoine's actions in this scenario?				

CASE 53: CTRL-C/CTRL-V

Anika is a BCBA supervising Yoshiko, a Board Certified Assistant Behavior Analyst (BCaBA), accumulating supervised hours toward her BCBA credential. Anika and Yoshiko follow the BACB's Task List and consistently document their experience and supervision hours. While meeting, Anika provides Yoshiko with her time-saving strategies and tips for maintaining a caseload. Anika shows Yoshiko how she generates behavior support plans based on a learner's functioning from a skeleton template of previously developed plans that she has written. Anika matches the function with the correct initial generic template and adds the learner's name and initiation date to the already developed behavior plan, allowing her to complete the support plan in less time. Once implemented, she may make adjustments to the plan, if necessary.

Applicable Ethics Code(s):				
Rationale for Chosen Code(s):				
Code Violation?	Yes	No	Need More Information	If Situation Continues
Antecedent Factors Contributing to Scenario:				
Preventative Strategies:				
Ethical Course of Action:				
Future Risk Factors to Keep in Mind:				
Discussion Questions:				
How might Yoshika's response to the ethical scenario differ from Anika's? How might they be similar?				

CASE 54: RUNNING ON EMPTY

Aki is a BCBA who recently started providing services to a new learner who was transferred from another agency. After reviewing the learner's records, Aki observed that the learner's most recent behavior support plan targeting reduction of aggressive behaviors included contingent exercise (i.e., one lap around his house whenever he aggresses). The data Aki has been provided demonstrate a reduction of aggressive behaviors coinciding with the initiation of the current plan. Aki decides to continue the behavior support plan as written to ease the transition to the new agency and staff.

Applicable Ethics Code(s):	2.01 Providing effective treatment			
Rationale for Chosen Code(s):				
This treatment is a punishment. This BCBA is not providing effective or useful interventions.				
Code Violation?	Yes	No	Need More Information	If Situation Continues
Antecedent Factors Contributing to Scenario:				
Preventative Strategies:				
Ethical Course of Action:				
Future Risk Factors to Keep in Mind:				
Discussion Questions:				
Would your responses change if the previous service provider submitted their data regarding previously attempted behavioral strategies prior to the implementation of contingent exercise?				

CASE 55: SWEET TOOTH

Meredith is a BCBA supervising the intervention of Mai, a 19-year-old learner diagnosed with a DD. Staff are having an extremely difficult time increasing Mai's participation in programs. Meredith conducted a preference assessment since the staff have reported that they "cannot find anything to get Mai to attend during teaching sessions." The assessment shows that Mai's highest preferred items include fast food and candy. Meredith has begun integrating these items as reinforcers within Mai's treatment.

Applicable Ethics Code(s):				
Rationale for Chosen Code(s):				
Code Violation?	Yes	No	Need More Information	If Situation Continues
Antecedent Factors Contributing to Scenario:				
Preventative Strategies:				
Ethical Course of Action:				
Future Risk Factors to Keep in Mind:				
Discussion Questions:				
What ethical challenges might Meredith encounter if she were to not include any of Mai's preferred items as potential reinforcers?				

CASE 56: PUNITIVE MEASURES

Olivia works as a BCBA at an ABA agency with several other BCBAs on staff. Often, if one of her colleagues is sick or on vacation, arrangements are made for supervision coverage with the other BCBAs. Olivia has been asked to cover Jaylan's cases while he is off for the week. While reviewing a behavior plan at a team meeting for one of Jaylan's cases, Olivia notices little documentation or direction for how the staff members should respond if the learner engages in a replacement behavior. The behavior plan only specifically states that staff should sternly say "No!" and use response-blocking techniques should the learner engage in a targeted challenging behavior.

Applicable Ethics Code(s):				
Rationale for Chosen Code(s):				
Code Violation?	Yes	No	Need More Information	If Situation Continues
Antecedent Factors Contributing to Scenario:				
Preventative Strategies:				
Ethical Course of Action:				
Future Risk Factors to Keep in Mind:				
Discussion Questions:				
What might help Olivia identify whether an ethical violation has occurred in this scenario?				

CASE 57: LET'S MOVE

Lana is a BCBA supervising the behavioral intervention of an adult, Marcus, diagnosed with a DD. Staff have reported that whenever they give a directive to participate in new activities, Marcus begins to bite his hand. The biting has become so severe that Marcus now has constant grooves and red marks on his skin and has required bandages on several occasions. As part of her assessment, Lana asked Marcus's parents if they had also observed hand biting. Similar to the staff members' reports, it appears that Marcus engages in the behavior when asked to perform new or nonpreferred activities. Based on her assessments and discussion with the staff and parents, Lana develops a behavior intervention plan to reduce hand biting maintained by contingent escape. Lana includes several proactive strategies to prevent the likelihood of the behavior occurring and incorporates reactive strategies for managing the behavior should it occur. The behavior plan also implements strategies that promote appropriate replacement behaviors. Given the significant nature of the behavior and that Marcus has already caused damage to his skin that may be long-lasting, Lana implements the behavior plan at her observation session the following day. She intends to review and discuss the plan with Marcus and his family at the team meeting later in the week.

Applicable Ethics Code(s):				
Rationale for Chosen Code(s):				
Code Violation?	Yes	No	Need More Information	If Situation Continues
Antecedent Factors Contributing to Scenario:				
Preventative Strategies:				
Ethical Course of Action:				
Future Risk Factors to Keep in Mind:				

CASE 58: ALL IN THE FAMILY

Mike is an RBT who provides services within the home of Miguel, a 10-year-old boy diagnosed with ASD. Miguel has two younger brothers, ages 6 and 4, living in the home. The younger brothers often play in the vicinity of the session, sometimes joining in for different activities. Mike normally doesn't take issue and is usually able to practice a lot of social skills, sibling play, and coping and tolerance with the brothers. Recently though, the parents will leave Mike alone with all three brothers for 20–30 min at a time while they go inside and make dinner, do household chores, or take phone calls. Mike often feels like he is "babysitting" all three boys rather than holding an intervention session with Miguel.

Applicable Ethics Code(s):				
Rationale for Chosen Code(s):				
Code Violation?	Yes	No	Need More Information	If Situation Continues
Antecedent Factors Contributing to Scenario:				
Preventative Strategies:				
Ethical Course of Action:				
Future Risk Factors to Keep in Mind:				
Discussion Questions:				
What could Mike's supervisor do given the situation?				
What if Mike's supervisor advises him to, "Just do what you can with all the kids?"				

CASE 59: COMMUNITY INTEGRATION

Sierra is an RBT working with a 17-year-old learner within the home setting. A major aspect of the learner's current programming goals focuses on social interaction and comfort within the community. After several months of the learner's parents not planning or participating in community outings, Ling, the supervising BCBA, discussed the importance of increasing community opportunities and addressed the lack of progress on related goals. The family addressed any challenges and agreed to increase community outings. The first experience at a local hangout was very successful, leading to several additional community sessions at various locations, many at the request of the parents. While Sierra has noticed several positive developments with the increased outings, she is also aware that only a small portion of the actual time spent on these trips is dedicated toward program goals, with the rest spent waiting for the parents to complete their personal errands.

Applicable Ethics Code(s):				
Rationale for Chosen Code(s):				
Code Violation?	Yes	No	Need More Information	If Situation Continues
Antecedent Factors Contributing to Scenario:				
Preventative Strategies:				
Ethical Course of Action:				
Future Risk Factors to Keep in Mind:				
Discussion Questions:				
Would this be less concerning if the RBT was exceptionally talented at capturing learning opportunities in any setting, even during the errands?				

CASE 60: SUPPLIES WITH LEGS

Juanita is one of three RBTs working within the home of Ishmael, a young child with an intellectual disability. Her agency provides supplies for use during intervention sessions, including games, flashcards, and various toys. The materials are stored in a suggested location in the family's home so that the behavior technicians can access the items during their sessions. All of the materials are marked with the agency's name with the intention of being returned to the agency after the supplies are no longer needed for intervention purposes. Over the last several weeks, Juanita has noticed different items missing from the supply box. The other RBTs working within the home have noticed the same issue. Juanita mentioned the missing supplies to Ishmael's parents. After a very brief discussion, she was asked to leave the house before her session was complete.

Applicable Ethics Code(s) :				
Rationale for Chosen Code(s):				
Code Violation?	Yes	No	Need More Information	If Situation Continues
Antecedent Factors Contributing to Scenario:				
Preventative Strategies:				
Ethical Course of Action:				
Future Risk Factors to Keep in Mind:				
Discussion Questions:				
How might your response change if Ishmael's parents said they do not have any other toys that he enjoys playing with during the times when Juanita and the rest of his team are not at the home?				

CASE 61: ALL BOOKED UP

Sylvie is a BCBA working with Ravonna, a 3-year-old diagnosed with ASD. Based on assessment results, interviews and observations conducted, strengths identified, and areas of need detected, Sylvie has developed a treatment plan with individualized goals and objectives. Sylvie recommends 30 hours per week of direct behavioral intervention to appropriately work toward the items included within the intervention plan. Ravonna's parents have reviewed the intervention plan and approve of all of the focus areas; however, they informed Sylvie that Ravonna would only be available to participate in 10 hours per week of intervention.

Applicable Ethics Code(s):				
Rationale for Chosen Code(s):				
Code Violation?	Yes	No	Need More Information	If Situation Continues
Antecedent Factors Contributing to Scenario:				
Preventative Strategies:				
Ethical Course of Action:				
Future Risk Factors to Keep in Mind:				
Discussion Questions:				
Would your recommendations of how Sylvie should proceed change if Ravonna's limited availability was due to either her attendance in a daycare program, her participation in equine therapy, or due to her parent's apprehension for Ravonna's participation in a comprehensive ABA program?				
What ethical and clinical considerations would you recommend Sylvie take if she were to continue working with Ravonna at the available 10 hours per week of direct ABA intervention?				
What factors would you recommend Sylvie consider if she were to determine that she could not work with Ravonna given Ravonna's limited availability?				

CASE 62: UNLOCKED AND UNLOADED

During her home-based session with Dwight, an RBT, Jodi, saw a handgun placed on a high shelf in Dwight's parents' office. Although the firearm was directly out of reach to Dwight, it could still be accessed if he stood on the chair in the office. It did not appear the handgun was locked in a safe while on the shelf. Jodi immediately asked Dwight's parents if they were aware of the gun and if they could place the gun in a secured location. Jodi was told not to worry about the gun since the family keeps the bullets in a separate location.

Applicable Ethics Code(s):				
Rationale for Chosen Code(s):				
Code Violation?	Yes	No	Need More Information	If Situation Continues
Antecedent Factors Contributing to Scenario:				
Preventative Strategies:				
Ethical Course of Action:				
Future Risk Factors to Keep in Mind:				
Discussion Questions:				
How might you suggest Jodi immediately address the situation?				
If you were the BCBA supervising Dwight's ABA services, how might you proceed in working with the family if they did not plan to place the gun in a secured location during home-based sessions?				

CASE 63: CAN YOU HEAR ME NOW?

Celia is a BCBA working with an ABA agency in a small rural town. One of her current learners and their family are moving significantly farther away from the agency's office location. Despite the distance, Celia's agency is still the closest service provider. However, given the distance, Celia is unable to find staff who can consistently travel to the learner's home, and the family has safety concerns with driving the learner to the agency's office. Celia has extensive experience delivering services via telehealth modalities and determined that continued service through video streaming would be an appropriate option for this learner. After several in-person trainings with the learner's parents, Celia transitions to telehealth sessions. Unfortunately, as a result of the home's poor internet, each session has been interrupted due to dropped connections and choppy feeds.

Applicable Ethics Code(s):				
Rationale for Chosen Code(s):				
Code Violation?	Yes	No	Need More Information	If Situation Continues
Antecedent Factors Contributing to Scenario:				
Preventative Strategies:				
Ethical Course of Action:				
Future Risk Factors to Keep in Mind:				

CASE 64: ZOOMING INTO TREATMENT

Due to health and safety concerns, James, an 11-year-old diagnosed with ASD, is not able to participate in face-to-face ABA services. James has consistently benefited from his involvement in his ABA program. He has shown an increase across skill development targets and an overall reduction in aggressive and self-injurious behaviors within sessions. Darlene, the BCBA working with James, would like to continue to provide ABA services. She has asked James's parents to switch to participating in telehealth services in which one of the parents would sit with James at the computer while Darlene implements James's current treatment protocols and programs through a video platform. During the telehealth sessions, James's parents will be expected to ensure all supplies are available and redirect any interfering behaviors. Given the immediacy of the health concern, Darlene plans to train James's parents to address and minimize dangerous behaviors, as these continue to occur in the home setting without staff present during their first several telehealth sessions.

Applicable Ethics Code(s):				
Rationale for Chosen Code(s):				
Code Violation?	Yes	No	Need More Information	If Situation Continues
Antecedent Factors Contributing to Scenario:				
Preventative Strategies:				
Ethical Course of Action:				
Future Risk Factors to Keep in Mind:				

CASE 65: PROMISES, PROMISES

Ailani, a BCBA, has started providing services to a new learner at her ABA agency. The learner had received behavioral services prior to starting with Ailani's agency but stopped due to a change in available funding. The learner's previous program was based on the procedures of Floortime. Ailani met with the parents and discussed ABA services and her agency's foundation and approach. The parents were very invested and interested but were also very happy with their previous agency and were apprehensive about all the changes. Ailani assured the parents that she would be heavily involved in the transition and provide as much parent education and support as possible. She also promised to integrate the preferred aspects of the learner's previous treatment plan and strategies to ease the change and appease the parents.

Applicable Ethics Code(s):				
Rationale for Chosen Code(s):				
Code Violation?	Yes	No	Need More Information	If Situation Continues
Antecedent Factors Contributing to Scenario:				
Preventative Strategies:				
Ethical Course of Action:				
Future Risk Factors to Keep in Mind:				
Discussion Questions:				
Would your concern with incorporating some aspects of Floortime wane if some of the procedures identified as Floortime were behavioral?				

Chapter 7

Section 3: Responsibility to Clients and Stakeholders

Behavior analysts have the dual responsibility of establishing themselves in their work and representing others who call themselves behavior analysts (Bailey & Burch, 2016). As such, in accordance with the individual needs of the client, behavior analysts are expected to support, advocate for, and educate learners and stakeholders about appropriate intervention and assessment based in applied behavior analysis (ABA).

Although not often reported due to lack of awareness, the American Psychological Association (2018) notes that many of the most common ethical violations to the APA Ethics Code, which is similar to the Behavior Analyst Certification Board Ethics Code (BACB, 2020b), relate directly to a practitioner's responsibility to the clients to whom they provide services. Section 3 of the BACB Ethics Code emphasizes behavior analysts' continued commitment toward representing the field of ABA with integrity and their responsibility toward those who may be affected by their involvement when implementing evidence-based, behavior-change assessment and intervention (BACB, 2020b). The four most common violations noted by the APA, three of which are directly noted within Section 3 of the BACB Code, include (1) maintaining confidentiality, (2) navigating potential multiple relationships, (3) discontinuing intervention, and (4) recommending and implementing research-based, effective intervention strategies.

Although a thorough and comprehensive discussion on this topic may be beyond the scope of this workbook, alternative interventions, sometimes referred to as "fad treatments," continue to increase in popularity and presence. As the number of individuals diagnosed with autism spectrum disorder (ASD) continues to rise, the number of interventions associated with the condition will also likely become more prominent. Although they often do not have any empirical support, fad treatments remain popular due to their implied association with other well-researched forms of intervention, claims of success, use of anecdotal reports, endorsements by celebrities, and easy access to those that may be enticed by their possibilities (Zane et al., 2008). Unfortunately, while practicing behavior analysts may differentiate between efficacious interventions and troubling alternatives, many within the general public continue to be tempted by the claims made by fad treatments. We suggest further reading related to the allure (Smith & Wick, 2008), identification (Finn et al., 2005; National Autism

Center, 2009, 2015; Smith & Wick, 2008), and cost (Zane et al., 2008) of fad treatments. While it may not be the responsibility of all those working within the field of ABA to confront or correct misinterpretations or misunderstandings held by those outside the field, by maintaining an ethically appropriate and conceptually systematic approach, behavior analysts may be better adept at responding to inaccurate viewpoints (Schlinger, 2015).

CASE 66: UNFORTUNATE NEWS

Naomi is a Registered Behavior Technician (RBT) providing services within the school setting. A student within Naomi's class has come to school each day with several new bruises. Naomi and the classroom teacher discuss their concerns related to the student and determine, based on the bruises and some additional background information, that they have a reasonable suspicion that the child may be a victim of physical abuse. Naomi and the teacher have talked about their beliefs related to the abuse but have not discussed whether either of them would report the abuse to the proper authorities. Given that the teacher is ultimately responsible for the well-being of the classroom and holds greater authority, Naomi presumes that the teacher will make the abuse report.

Applicable Ethics Code(s):				
Rationale for Chosen Code(s):				
Code Violation?	Yes	No	Need More Information	If Situation Continues
Antecedent Factors Contributing to Scenario:				
Preventative Strategies:				
Ethical Course of Action:				
Future Risk Factors to Keep in Mind:				
Discussion Questions:				
Do you agree with Naomi's presumption? If not, why?				
What ethical obligation does Naomi have if she suspects child abuse?				
Does Naomi have an ethical obligation to report the suspected child abuse even if the teacher has reported it?				

CASE 67: SHORT STAFFED

Richard's family is eager to start ABA services. They have contacted Barbara, a Board Certified Behavior Analyst (BCBA), and have begun the intake process. After conducting assessments and observations and developing an intervention plan, Barbara identified Richard would benefit from a comprehensive 30 hour per week behavioral intervention program. At this time, Barbara's ABA agency does not have staff available to meet the recommended intensity of service. However, she believes she may be able to hire new staff members in the near future and increase the service hours provided. As a result, Barbara informed Richard's family that she recommends starting services immediately at 15 hour per week of direct instruction.

Applicable Ethics Code(s):				
Rationale for Chosen Code(s):				
Code Violation?	Yes	No	Need More Information	If Situation Continues
Antecedent Factors Contributing to Scenario:				
Preventative Strategies:				
Ethical Course of Action:				
Future Risk Factors to Keep in Mind:				
Discussion Questions:				
Do you believe the ethical concerns involved in the scenario would change if there were other ABA agencies within the geographic area who had the staffing available to provide more intensive services? If so, what is Barbara's ethical obligation in discussing the start of services with the family?				

CASE 68: FIXER UPPER

Hernando is a BCBA who provides direct services and intervention planning for a small number of learners within his independent private practice. While conducting a session at Phillip's house, Hernando's car was hit by another driver causing slight damage to the door. Phillip's father happened to be a mechanic and was able to repair the dent and fix the scratches while Hernando completed his session with Phillip. Hernando thanked Phillip's father for his help. Phillip's father said it was not a problem and that he would be willing to fix any other damages and conduct regular maintenance on Hernando's car in exchange for a reduction in Hernando's fee for working with Phillip.

Applicable Ethics Code(s):				
Rationale for Chosen Code(s):				
Code Violation?	Yes	No	Need More Information	If Situation Continues
Antecedent Factors Contributing to Scenario:				
Preventative Strategies:				
Ethical Course of Action:				
Future Risk Factors to Keep in Mind:				
Discussion Questions:				
Under what conditions do you believe Hernando and Phillip's father's arrangement would be more or less appropriate?				

CASE 69: PAUSED PAYMENTS

Shira receives ABA services from Behavior Interventions, Inc. Without the ABA agency's knowledge, Shira's mother's company changed insurance providers. As a result, Shira has not had an active authorization in place for the last 4 months. Behavior Interventions, Inc. does not accept the new insurance and has informed Shira's family that they will be discontinuing services in 2 weeks assuming no other funding source is identified.

Applicable Ethics Code(s):				
Rationale for Chosen Code(s):				
Code Violation?	Yes	No	Need More Information	If Situation Continues
Antecedent Factors Contributing to Scenario:				
Preventative Strategies:				
Ethical Course of Action:				
Future Risk Factors to Keep in Mind:				

CASE 70: ON CALL

Rosario is a doctoral-level BCBA (BCBA-D) who oversees the ABA services for Tiara, an adolescent diagnosed with ASD. Tiara's mother recently informed Rosario that Tiara will be starting two new medications, as prescribed by her pediatrician, with a focus on reducing "irritability" and "behavior challenges." Rosario has a signed release of information to communicate with Tiara's pediatrician but has not yet collaborated or introduced herself to initiate contact.

Applicable Ethics Code(s):				
Rationale for Chosen Code(s):				
Code Violation?	Yes	No	Need More Information	If Situation Continues
Antecedent Factors Contributing to Scenario:				
Preventative Strategies:				
Ethical Course of Action:				
Future Risk Factors to Keep in Mind:				

Discussion Questions:

Would Rosario's ethical obligations or course of action change if she had learned Tiara had already been taking the prescribed medication for several months?

Would Rosario's ethical obligations or course of action change if instead of medication it was recommended that Tiara be placed on a special diet or to start taking an herbal supplement?

CASE 71: STAY IN MY LANE

Maryam is a BCBA providing supervisory ABA services to Xavier, a young learner diagnosed with ASD, as funded through the family's insurance provider. Maryam has been working with Xavier for about 1 year within the home setting. In addition to the ABA services provided through Maryam's company, Xavier receives Occupational Therapy and Speech Therapy within the school setting. He is also supported by a behavioral aide funded by his school district who is supervised by the district's BCBA. Maryam is aware of Xavier's classroom arrangement and supportive services and has offered to attend Individual Education Plan (IEP) meetings at the school. However, since she only oversees Xavier's home programming, she has not attempted to contact any of the other professionals working with Xavier and has not approached his family for a release of information to collaborate and consult.

Applicable Ethics Code(s):				
Rationale for Chosen Code(s):				
Code Violation?	Yes	No	Need More Information	If Situation Continues
Antecedent Factors Contributing to Scenario:				
Preventative Strategies:				
Ethical Course of Action:				
Future Risk Factors to Keep in Mind:				
Discussion Questions:				
Do Maryam's ethical obligations differ since Xavier receives support from another BCBA?				
How might Maryam maintain her ethical responsibilities if Xavier's family is not comfortable signing a release of information?				

CASE 72: RIGHTS TO RESULTS

Reba, a BCBA, has been contracted by the local school district to conduct a Functional Behavior Assessment (FBA) and adaptive skills assessment on a high school student currently receiving ABA services through the school. Reba met with the student and interviewed the parents, school personnel, and treatment providers as well as conducted several comprehensive direct and indirect assessments. Following her evaluation, Reba completed her report and reviewed her assessments with the student's parents. The parents were very concerned and felt that the school may decrease services after receiving Reba's results. They asked that she not share the report with the school. Reba informed the parents that she was contracted by the school to complete the assessment and would have to provide her results. The parents were not aware that because the school funded Reba's assessment they were entitled to the report.

Applicable Ethics Code(s):				
Rationale for Chosen Code(s):				
Code Violation?	Yes	No	Need More Information	If Situation Continues
Antecedent Factors Contributing to Scenario:				
Preventative Strategies:				
Ethical Course of Action:				
Future Risk Factors to Keep in Mind:				
Discussion Questions:				
What codes might apply if the student's parents independently contracted with Reba to conduct the assessment and the school was requesting the results?				

CASE 73: YOU GET WHAT YOU GET

Destiny, a BCBA, has submitted a treatment plan and authorization request of 25 hours per week of ABA services, along with additional hours for supervision and caregiver training for Keven, a 6-year-old diagnosed with ASD. After reviewing the request with Keven's funding organization, Destiny is informed that she has been authorized for 10 hours of the requested 25 hours per week of direct instruction. Destiny has appealed the determination. However, the funding organization upheld the determination, and the available funded hours have remained the same.

Applicable Ethics Code(s):				
Rationale for Chosen Code(s):				
Code Violation?	Yes	No	Need More Information	If Situation Continues
Antecedent Factors Contributing to Scenario:				
Preventative Strategies:				
Ethical Course of Action:				
Future Risk Factors to Keep in Mind:				

CASE 74: REASONABLE SUSPICION

Monty, a BCBA, has reasonable suspicion that one of the learners he works with may be the victim of child abuse. Upon receiving this information, he immediately contacts Child Protective Services and completes the necessary steps in filing a child abuse report. About 1 week later, Monty receives an irate phone call from the learner's parents. While they do not know for sure that Monty filed the abuse report, they believe he was the one who made the call. The parents stated they were never told their information could be shared with others for any reason and believed their identities would be protected under any circumstance.

Applicable Ethics Code(s):				
Rationale for Chosen Code(s):				
Code Violation?	Yes	No	Need More Information	If Situation Continues
Antecedent Factors Contributing to Scenario:				
Preventative Strategies:				
Ethical Course of Action:				
Future Risk Factors to Keep in Mind:				
Discussion Questions:				
Assuming Monty did not inform the learner's parents at any point about how and when their information may be shared with others, does this mean Monty is no longer in a position to contact appropriate services when he is aware of potential abuse?				

CASE 75: FIGHTING FADS

LaTonya is a BCBA providing services to a teenage girl, Tia, diagnosed with ASD. Progress has been slow, but the team has managed to make some consistent improvements. The parents are very involved in team meetings and in behavioral intervention sessions. However, they often discuss how frustrated they are with their daughter's challenges. While LaTonya is empathetic to the family's concerns, she believes that the team is making the right clinical decisions based on the data and the learner's level of need. Recently, at a team meeting, Tia's parents mentioned that they heard about the success of using hyperbaric oxygen chamber therapy for individuals with ASD and are thinking about taking Tia to receive the treatment.

Applicable Ethics Code(s):				
Rationale for Chosen Code(s):				
Code Violation?	Yes	No	Need More Information	If Situation Continues
Antecedent Factors Contributing to Scenario:				
Preventative Strategies:				
Ethical Course of Action:				
Future Risk Factors to Keep in Mind:				
Discussion Questions:				
How might LaTonya's response change if Tia's parents have already begun hyperbaric oxygen treatments?				

CASE 76: STAY THE COURSE

Hunter is a BCBA who was recently hired at an ABA clinic. When reviewing his new caseload with the office manager, Bella, who is not a BCBA, Hunter is told that all of the learners he will be working with receive behavioral intervention for 40 hours per week. Bella informs Hunter that a 40 hour program is consistent with the clinic's service model and helps with scheduling and billing. Bella tells Hunter that he is free to recommend whatever he thinks is appropriate, but any changes to the clinic model would "probably create some challenges and confusion."

Applicable Ethics Code(s):				
Rationale for Chosen Code(s):				
Code Violation?	Yes	No	Need More Information	If Situation Continues
Antecedent Factors Contributing to Scenario:				
Preventative Strategies:				
Ethical Course of Action:				
Future Risk Factors to Keep in Mind:				
Discussion Questions:				
Under what circumstances would it be ethically appropriate for Hunter to continue to recommend a 40 hour per week program for his cases?				
Under what conditions would a 40 hour per week recommendation not be ethically appropriate?				

CASE 77: PUT WORDS IN YOUR MOUTH

Terrence is a 22-year-old, nonverbal man diagnosed with ASD. Brennan is the BCBA supervising Terrence's behavioral intervention program. Terrence uses an Augmentative and Alternative Communication (AAC) device in the form of a tablet to communicate. Brennan consistently coordinates with Terrence's Speech–Language Pathologist (SLP) to support Terrence's use of the device. Brennan recently learned from the SLP that Terrence's parents hired an additional speech coach to work with Terrence. Brennan observed a training session between Terrence and the new speech coach, who informed Brennan that Terrence's communication has "exploded" since using their new system. In her observation, Brennan noticed the speech coach placing a keyboard in front of Terrence and lightly guiding his arm to press the different keys.

Applicable Ethics Code(s):				
Rationale for Chosen Code(s):				
Code Violation?	Yes	No	Need More Information	If Situation Continues
Antecedent Factors Contributing to Scenario:				
Preventative Strategies:				
Ethical Course of Action:				
Future Risk Factors to Keep in Mind:				
Discussion Questions:				
Does Brennan's ethical responsibility toward Terrence and his family change if she does not incorporate the new speech system within sessions with Terrence?				
Do you suggest Brennan speak with Terrence's parents regarding the new speech system? If so, how would you suggest she approach the family?				

CASE 78: NONESSENTIAL OILS

At a parent meeting, Lisette, a BCBA, is informed by the parents of Pearl, a 7-year-old diagnosed with ASD, that the family has begun giving Pearl regular doses of cannabidiol (CBD) oil. The parents heard about the supposed benefits of CBD oil for children diagnosed with ASD from friends and ordered the oil from the Internet. According to the parents, Pearl receives a few drops of the oil in the mornings and a few more in the afternoon. Though they have not noticed any change yet, they are hopeful that the oil will help increase Pearl's communication and general response to her ABA services. Pearl's parents have notified her pediatrician about the change and told Lisette she is welcome to speak with the doctor at any time.

Applicable Ethics Code(s):				
Rationale for Chosen Code(s):				
Code Violation?	Yes	No	Need More Information	If Situation Continues
Antecedent Factors Contributing to Scenario:				
Preventative Strategies:				
Ethical Course of Action:				
Future Risk Factors to Keep In Mind:				
Discussion Questions:				
How might Lisette's response or ethical responsibilities change if, rather than CBD oil, Pearl's parents were giving her oils with tetrahydrocannabinol (THC), the main psychoactive compound in marijuana?				

CASE 79: LOOK NO FURTHER

Conner is a BCBA-D and specializes in providing services for adolescents and young adults with ASD and other DDs. Within his practice, Conner uses behavioral intervention strategies to assist with high school and college transitions, job skills, and independent living needs. Silas, a learner to whom Conner provides services, has shared feelings of depression and thoughts related to self-harm and suicide. Conner has confirmed that Silas does not have an active plan or reliable means to hurt himself. Though Conner has established a strong therapeutic rapport with Silas, he feels his training and expertise are inadequate to ensure Silas's safety. Conner's office is next door to a licensed clinical psychologist. After obtaining the appropriate release of information, Conner has referred Silas to the licensed clinical psychologist next door.

Applicable Ethics Code(s):				
Rationale for Chosen Code(s):				
Code Violation?	Yes	No	Need More Information	If Situation Continues
Antecedent Factors Contributing to Scenario:				
Preventative Strategies:				
Ethical Course of Action:				
Future Risk Factors to Keep in Mind:				

CASE 80: MUFFIN MELODRAMA

Dr. Lorton is a developmental pediatrician who often conducts diagnostic assessments for individuals with a potential ASD diagnosis. He has several ABA agencies in his referral Rolodex. Jade is a BCBA-D who has received several recent referrals from Dr. Lorton. To show her appreciation and maintain the professional relationship, Jade has sent Dr. Lorton's office staff a basket of muffins along with a "Thank you" card.

Applicable Ethics Code(s):				
Rationale for Chosen Code(s):				
Code Violation?	Yes	No	Need More Information	If Situation Continues
Antecedent Factors Contributing to Scenario:				
Preventative Strategies:				
Ethical Course of Action:				
Future Risk Factors to Keep in Mind:				
Discussion Questions:				
Would your thoughts related to the applicable ethics code(s) change if Jade had only sent Dr.Lorton's office a "Thank you" card? What if she had sent a card with a gift certificate to a local restaurant?				

CASE 81: YOU SCRATCH MY BACK

Gabe, a BCBA, and Aaron, a physical therapist, are friends from college who both work in the same town. Aaron offered Gabe tickets to a sporting event, which he accepted. During the game, Gabe thanked Aaron for the great seats, to which Aaron replied, "No problem, consider it payback for all the great referrals you've been sending my way."

Applicable Ethics Code(s):				
Rationale for Chosen Code(s):				
Code Violation?	Yes	No	Need More Information	If Situation Continues
Antecedent Factors Contributing to Scenario:				
Preventative Strategies:				
Ethical Course of Action:				
Future Risk Factors to Keep in Mind:				
Discussion Questions:				
Was Gabe's acceptance of the ticket to the sporting event an ethical violation?				
Are there ethical implications associated with referring clients to friends?				

CASE 82: CUT OFF

Jocelyn is a BCBA-D and owns an ABA agency providing services for children, adolescents, and young adults diagnosed with ASD. Her agency has been working with Mason for almost 3 years, with services funded through Mason's mother's insurance. Mason's mother recently changed jobs and no longer has coverage through the same insurance company. Jocelyn's agency is not in-network with Mason's mother's new insurance provider. Mason has been making progress but would benefit from continued intervention. Mason's parents are concerned that they will no longer be able to afford Mason's services with Jocelyn's agency.

Applicable Ethics Code(s):				
Rationale for Chosen Code(s):				
Code Violation?	Yes	No	Need More Information	If Situation Continues
Antecedent Factors Contributing to Scenario:				
Preventative Strategies:				
Ethical Course of Action:				
Future Risk Factors to Keep in Mind:				

CASE 83: SHOULD I STAY OR SHOULD I GO

Chereika is a BCBA working within an ABA agency. She has been providing services to Troy for several years. Troy has made excellent progress, and based on the data and Chereika's clinical opinion, is ready to "graduate" from individual-based services with her agency. Chereika has already begun integrating community-based services, has increased her intervention focus to take advantage of natural learning opportunities, and is appropriately fading her team's clinical involvement. Though Chereika indicated her intention to discontinue services to Troy's funding organization, she received a new authorization to provide continued services at the same intensity. Chereika informed Troy's parents of the available funding for additional services. While they are proud and excited about Troy's progress, they appreciate the relationship Troy has built with Chereika and her staff and are very interested in the opportunity to continue services at the current intensity of hours through the duration of the new authorization.

Applicable Ethics Code(s):				
Rationale for Chosen Code(s):				
Code Violation?	Yes	No	Need More Information	If Situation Continues
Antecedent Factors Contributing to Scenario:				
Preventative Strategies:				
Ethical Course of Action:				
Future Risk Factors to Keep in Mind:				

Section 4: Responsibility to Supervisees and Trainees

The term "supervision," as commonly utilized by those who practice within the field of applied behavior analysis (ABA), has come to reference two similar, yet distinct activities and responsibilities. Dependent on context, the term may be used to relate to *Trainee Supervision*, which references the oversite of Board Certified Behavior Analyst (BCBA) candidates in accruing the necessary experience hours and training toward sitting for the BCBA certification exam.

"Supervision," as a standalone label, may also indicate a behavior analyst's activities of *Clinical Supervision*, denoting their overall accountability of the direction for the assessment and intervention for learners to whom they have identified their role as the responsible clinician.

Prior to the release of the current Behavior Analyst Certification Board (2020b), trainee and clinical supervision were both referenced within the same portion of the Code. It is understandable to equate both supervisory activities not only in title but also in relation to ethical responsibilities, as most direct implementation of intervention procedures within behavior-analytic programs is not typically conducted by behavior analysts themselves. Instead, a BCBA may oversee the activities of other supervised professionals, such as Registered Behavior Technicians (RBTs) or Board Certified Assistant Behavior Analysts (BCaBAs). As a result, behavior analysts are responsible for the development of procedures and data collection methods, as well as whether these processes are carried out appropriately and effectively by those under the BCBA's guidance. Given this, clinical supervisors have potentially the most important responsibility within the field of ABA, as not only are they accountable for the direction of intervention, but through that care, they essentially determine the public's impression of ABA as a field. Perhaps in relation to the potential ramification of clinical supervision, the current Code has dispersed aspects of clinical supervisory responsibilities and incorporated expectations throughout multiple sections of the Code.

While the impact of appropriate and ethical clinical supervision cannot and should not be dismissed, all BCBAs have at some point in their career been directly involved with the trainee supervision process. As a requirement to sit for the BCBA certification exam, all candidates must have participated in clinical experience hours supervised by a BCBA.

A Workbook of Ethical Case Scenarios in Applied Behavior Analysis, Second Edition. https://doi.org/10.1016/B978-0-323-98813-1.00001-3

Those who have become supervisors of trainees have varying experiences and histories of learning. Therefore, their practices, approaches, and priorities as supervisors are likely to be influenced by their own experience as a trainee (Leblanc et al., 2020a,b). As a result, beneficial strategies may be continued, but it is equally possible that unethical or harmful supervisory practices will be inherited and passed down (Sellers et al., 2016a). Thus, a cycle of unwitting liabilities may be created and continued, impacting future generations of behavior analysts and individuals they serve.

Many behavior analysts become supervisors either of trainees or of intervention programs very early in their independent professional career, increasing the potential of ethical challenges and questionable practices. To combat the greater likelihood of ethical issues and better ensure that quality training and experience is passed down from supervisor to trainee, it is imperative that supervisors and trainees clearly state at the outset of the supervisory relationship the expectations of both parties. Such assertions should include the basic structure of BCBA supervision and agreements related to the provision and acceptance of (1) constructive feedback and criticism, (2) consistent evaluation strategies, (3) skill development activities and assessments, (4) expected learning goals, and (5) strategies for assessing and managing barriers within supervision (Sellers et al., 2016b,c).

CASE 84: SPREAD TOO THIN

Kimiko is a BCBA supervising several BCaBAs and RBTs working toward accruing experience hours to take their BCBA exam. Kimiko and her agency are very passionate about supporting the growth of ABA and follow a strong policy of promoting and hiring from within the agency as much as possible. As a result, many of the direct staff members have inquired about joining ABA graduate programs and gaining supervision from Kimiko. While Kimiko wants to support her staff, she is having trouble dividing her time between providing supervision and maintaining her caseload. Kimiko brought up her concerns with the agency's clinical director, who assured her that as more of the staff become certified themselves, they will be able to take on more cases and relieve some of Kimiko's clinical responsibilities. Though this may prove to be helpful in the future, Kimiko is currently struggling to appropriately dedicate her time to her required tasks.

Applicable Ethics Code(s):				
Rationale for Chosen Code(s):				
Code Violation?	Yes	No	Need More Information	If Situation Continues
Antecedent Factors Contributing to Scenario:				
Preventative Strategies:				
Ethical Course of Action:				
Future Risk Factors to Keep in Mind:				
Discussion Questions:				
How might Kimiko's response to the situation change if her clinical director is not a BCBA?				

CASE 85: SLIPPERY SUPERVISION

Emilia and Sophia are both accruing supervised experience hours toward acquiring eligibility to sit for the BCBA exam. While Emilia and her supervisor are diligent about meeting consistently and tracking Emilia's experience, Sophia and her supervisor meet on an inconsistent basis and do not have a formal system for maintaining their records. Emilia and Sophia would like to submit their experience verification forms to the Behavior Analyst Certification Board (BACB) to take the exam. Emilia's forms are prepared and verified; however, Sophia has to go back through all her forms to finish preparing the ones that are missing and still need to be signed by her supervisor. Sophia has asked Emilia to help her complete her forms based on what Sophia recalls of her experiences.

Applicable Ethics Code(s):				
Rationale for Chosen Code(s):				
Code Violation?	Yes	No	Need More Information	If Situation Continues
Antecedent Factors Contributing to Scenario:				
Preventative Strategies:				
Ethical Course of Action:				
Future Risk Factors to Keep in Mind:				
Discussion Questions:				
What are the possible repercussions should Emilia agree to assist Sophia in completing her forms?				

CASE 86: FRACTURED FOCUS

Leia is a student accruing experience hours toward taking her BCBA exam. Her supervisor is a BCBA as well as a licensed clinical psychologist. During their allotted supervision meetings, Leia's supervisor spends the majority of their time discussing the automatic thoughts and core beliefs of their cases as opposed to the ABA-based programs implemented with learners.

Applicable Ethics Code(s):				
Rationale for Chosen Code(s):				
Code Violation?	Yes	No	Need More Information	If Situation Continues
Antecedent Factors Contributing to Scenario:				
Preventative Strategies:				
Ethical Course of Action:				
Future Risk Factors to Keep in Mind:				
Discussion Questions:				
Would the ethical implications be the same if Leia's supervisor discussed automatic thoughts and core beliefs with Leia in addition to their allotted supervision time spent discussing behaviour-analytic topics?				

CASE 87: COMPLIMENT SANDWICH

Misty is an RBT who is accruing supervised experience toward taking her BCBA exam with Bernadette, a BCBA. Though Misty and Bernadette both work for the same ABA agency and with the same learners, Misty expressed she feels she is rarely observed by Bernadette while working directly with learners. She is appreciative of the generally positive feedback she receives from Bernadette but states that she knows she "can't be doing everything right." Misty has spoken with Bernadette about her concerns and asked for more detailed and specific guidance and feedback about how she can grow, particularly related to the experiences she is expected to develop while accruing supervised hours.

Applicable Ethics Code(s):				
Rationale for Chosen Code(s):				
Code Violation?	Yes	No	Need More Information	If Situation Continues
Antecedent Factors Contributing to Scenario:				
Preventative Strategies:				
Ethical Course of Action:				
Future Risk Factors to Keep in Mind:				
Discussion Questions:				
Would Bernadette's ethical responsibilities change if she was Misty's assigned supervisor but the two were not working with the same learners at their ABA agency ?				

CASE 88: JUST DO IT

Wanda, a BCBA, is updating an intervention plan for a learner on her caseload to submit for insurance funding authorization. Part of the plan includes the completion of an adaptive assessment. Wanda will not have the opportunity to perform the assessment with the learner before the current authorization has expired. Agatha is Wanda's trainee who is also an RBT working with the learner. Agatha has the availability needed to conduct the assessment but does not have experience in conducting the assessment. Wanda instructs Agatha to complete the assessment and states that she will review the results and go over any of Agatha's questions upon completion.

Applicable Ethics Code(s):				
Rationale for Chosen Code(s):				
Code Violation?	Yes	No	Need More Information	If Situation Continues
Antecedent Factors Contributing to Scenario:				
Preventative Strategies:				
Ethical Course of Action:				
Future Risk Factors to Keep in Mind:				
Discussion Questions:				
How might the relevant ethics code(s) and potential violations be different if Agatha had some training and experience completing the assessment but had not yet done so without direct oversight by Wanda?				

Hector is a BCaBA receiving supervision toward sitting for his BCBA exam from Angel, a BCBA. Hector and Angel meet consistently, review Task List items, and engage in regular observations and feedback sessions. While Hector was working toward accumulating his supervised experience hours, Angel accepted a job offer to work with a different ABA agency. Since she is no longer working with the same learners or employed by the same agency, Angel has told Hector that once she officially leaves her position, she will no longer be able to provide him with supervisory support.

Applicable Ethics Code(s):				
Rationale for Chosen Code(s):				
Code Violation?	Yes	No	Need More Information	If Situation Continues
Antecedent Factors Contributing to Scenario:				
Preventative Strategies:				
Ethical Course of Action:				
Future Risk Factors to Keep in Mind:				
Discussion Questions:				
Do you think Angel's ethical obligations as a supervisor would be different if she was fired from her position at the company with Hector?				
Would Angel's responsibilities be different if she and Hector worked for a large ABA agency with many other BCBAs or a small agency with little to no other BCBAs?				

CASE 90: IN SEARCH OF SUPERVISION

Isabella is an RBT accruing supervision hours toward sitting for her BCBA exam. Her supervisor, Candice, works within the same agency. A close member of Candice's family recently passed away, and she has not been back to work for a little over 2 months. Isabella has attempted to remain in contact with Candice while Candice has been out on leave. This initially involved Isabella providing condolences, and eventually, it led to Isabella asking who will be taking over Candice's supervisory responsibilities. After not receiving a response following several attempts at contacting Candice, Isabella wrote to Candice using both her personal and work email addresses. In addition, Isabella asked other BCBAs at her agency what she should do and was told that their caseloads were too full to take on Candice's cases. Finally, Candice responded to Isabella's emails telling her to "stop worrying" and that she will "sign whatever supervision hours are needed" upon returning to the office.

Applicable Ethics Code(s):				
Rationale for Chosen Code(s):				
Code Violation?	Yes	No	Need More Information	If Situation Continues
Antecedent Factors Contributing to Scenario:				
Preventative Strategies:				
Ethical Course of Action:				
Future Risk Factors to Keep in Mind:				
Discussion Questions:				
Does Isabella have an obligation to secure an alternative source for supervision while Candice is away?				

Chapter 9

Section 5: Responsibility in Public Statements

Most individuals within the general public will not interact with applied behavior analysis (ABA) unless they come into contact directly with an individual who either provides services based in the science and principles of ABA or have a relationship with an individual or group who participates in behavior-analytic intervention. The active promotion and dissemination of ABA may help bridge the gap to those individuals who may not otherwise have a connection with ABA.

According to the Behavior Analyst Certification Board (2020b), *Public Statements* include

> *Delivery of information (digital or otherwise) in a public forum for the purpose of either better informing that audience or providing a call-to-action. This includes paid or unpaid advertising, brochures, printed material, directory listings, personal resumes or curriculum vitae, interviews, or comments for use in media (e.g., print, statements in legal proceedings, lectures and public presentations, social media, published materials) (p. 7).*

Given the wide variety of points of contact with the public, it becomes increasingly important for behavior analysts to ensure the information they impart is clear and accurate, based on behavior-analytic principles, and consistent with all areas of the Code (Kelly et al., 2019).

Overall, behavior analysts keeping with these recommendations are encouraged to promote their services as long as they do so in a responsible manner. Making false promises or deceptive claims, endorsing nonbehavioral strategies, or implying a therapeutic relationship where one does not exist, may result in devaluing the integrity of the individual making such claims and could hamper the public's impression of the field. Additionally, soliciting current clients for testimonials should also be avoided, yet unfortunately, recent research suggests that many agencies are out of compliance with this code by including client testimonials on their agency websites (Phu & Byrne, 2018).

Perhaps the quickest means of reaching the greatest audience for the dissemination of ABA is through social media. The number of private and publicly accessed social media groups related to ABA grows in membership and variety every day. However, while internet media sites help to forge connections and distribute content at a pace that was not previously possible through any other means, the risk of misinformation and misrepresentation has also grown exponentially. Sharing information related to a learner, providing clinical recommendations without proper assessment or knowledge of the scenario, and reliance on publicly shared advice rather than independently researching published empirical literature require significantly less response effort and can occur on a grander scale than ever before (O'Leary et al., 2017).

Though social media channels allow for greater access to both individuals and communities, behavior analysts must be cautious and should understand that any information shared, even on private sites, is available to the public and could ultimately reflect back on the behavior analyst and the field.

CASE 91: HEY, THAT'S ME!

Merritt is a Board Certified Behavior Analyst (BCBA) presenting research at a regional ABA conference. Within her presentation, she included several video examples of her research participants working with Registered Behavior Technicians (RBTs) implementing the teaching procedure being studied. Merritt received written releases of information to include video footage of the child participants but has not secured approvals from the RBTs.

Applicable Ethics Code(s):				
Rationale for Chosen Code(s):				
Code Violation?	Yes	No	Need More Information	If Situation Continues
Antecedent Factors Contributing to Scenario:				
Preventative Strategies:				
Ethical Course of Action:				
Future Risk Factors to Keep in Mind:				

Luca, a BCBA, is passionate about behavior analysis and about sharing the capabilities of the field with the public. He has established a large social media following using the handle "A-B-A-mazing." Through his various social media pages, Luca regularly posts short video content: (a) discussing particular aspects of behavior analytic strategies, (b) portraying interviews with members of the field, and (c) making creative memes and gifs with ABA topics and humor. Luca also allows others to post to his pages and will periodically share the graphics created by these other individuals. One meme shared by Luca, created by one of his followers, depicts a picture of an adult spraying a child with a water bottle with a caption that says, "RBT's be Like: Behavior Reduced. I'm Out." Luca received several comments from his followers expressing their concern about the content of the graphic.

Applicable Ethics Code(s):				
Rationale for Chosen Code(s):				
Code Violation?	Yes	No	Need More Information	If Situation Continues
Antecedent Factors Contributing to Scenario:				
Preventative Strategies:				
Ethical Course of Action:				
Future Risk Factors to Keep in Mind:				
Discussion Questions:				
Does Luca hold any responsibility for the meme since he did not actually create the graphic?				

CASE 93: TAKE MY ADVICE

Adam is a BCBA who gave a presentation at a local parent support group about parental participation in ABA programs. During the presentation, Adam received several questions from parents about strategies for supporting their children's progress and development. Adam answered the parents' questions to the best of his ability and provided suggestions and strategies for them to try at home. Several weeks later, Adam received a call from an attorney of one of the parents who attended the presentation. The attorney informed Adam that the parents were suing Adam because they attempted the strategies he suggested related to getting their child to consume new foods. As a result, the child required medical attention due to aspirating and is now resistant to eating any foods at all, including ones the child used to consume regularly.

Applicable Ethics Code(s):				
Rationale for Chosen Code(s):				
Code Violation?	Yes	No	Need More Information	If Situation Continues
Antecedent Factors Contributing to Scenario:				
Preventative Strategies:				
Ethical Course of Action:				
Future Risk Factors to Keep in Mind:				
Discussion Questions:				
Assuming the parents did not accurately follow Adam's recommendations as he described them during the presentation, does Adam hold any ethical responsibility in this circumstance?				

CASE 94: PROBLEMS IN PRESS

Elijah holds a doctorate degree in clinical psychology with a specialty in neuropsychological assessment; he is also a BCBA. Elijah was interviewed for a major news organization regarding the current prevalence rates of autism spectrum disorder (ASD). Upon review of the article, Elijah noticed that the author stated Elijah holds a doctorate degree in ABA.

Applicable Ethics Code(s):				
Rationale for Chosen Code(s):				
Code Violation?	Yes	No	Need More Information	If Situation Continues
Antecedent Factors Contributing to Scenario:				
Preventative Strategies:				
Ethical Course of Action:				
Future Risk Factors to Keep in Mind:				

CASE 95: PRESS RELEASE

Upon looking through her local newspaper, Harriet noticed an article written about the ABA adult day program where she works. In addition to covering the benefits of ABA for adults diagnosed with developmental disabilities (DD) in general, the article reported on Harriet's day program and provided their contact information. The article mentioned the success Harriet's day program has observed and distinguished the program's expertise from that of several other, specifically named, local ABA day programs. When Harriet arrived to work the next day, she noticed a pile of copies of the local paper available in the waiting room. Harriet's boss mentioned that she was very proud of the article and noted that she was originally going to buy a regular picture advertisement in the newspaper but was able to arrange with the editor to run a story about the agency instead for the same price.

Applicable Ethics Code(s):				
Rationale for Chosen Code(s):				
Code Violation?	Yes	No	Need More Information	If Situation Continues
Antecedent Factors Contributing to Scenario:				
Preventative Strategies:				
Ethical Course of Action:				
Future Risk Factors to Keep in Mind:				

CASE 96: PUBLIC PERSONA

Zara has a Master's degree in Business Administration (MBA) and is the Communications Director of an ABA agency owned by two doctoral-level Board Certified Behavior Analysts (BCBA-Ds). Along with managing the agency's marketing and promotional efforts, Zara maintains the agency's public relations image, which often includes giving interviews to media outlets as a representative of the agency. In her most recent interview, Zara is quoted as comparing ASD to diseases such as cancer and endorsing ABA-based intervention as an assured cure.

Applicable Ethics Code(s):				
Rationale for Chosen Code(s):				
Code Violation?	Yes	No	Need More Information	If Situation Continues
Antecedent Factors Contributing to Scenario:				
Preventative Strategies:				
Ethical Course of Action:				
Future Risk Factors to Keep in Mind:				
Discussion Questions:				
What is Zara's responsibility to the Code?				
Would you be less concerned with Zara's claims if she were to use the term "recover" instead of "cure?"				

CASE 97: DON'T QUOTE ME

Miguel is a BCBA who was interviewed by a prominent special needs parent blog. Miguel discussed the history and science of behavior analysis and its various applications. After a few weeks, the interview was posted on the blog's site. Upon reviewing the article, Miguel noticed that he was misquoted in several areas, especially related to the basic description of ABA.

Applicable Ethics Code(s):				
Rationale for Chosen Code(s):				
Code Violation?	Yes	No	Need More Information	If Situation Continues
Antecedent Factors Contributing to Scenario:				
Preventative Strategies:				
Ethical Course of Action:				
Future Risk Factors to Keep in Mind:				
Discussion Questions:				
Would Miguel's supervisor have any ethical obligations in this scenario if Miguel was a Board Certified Assistant Behavior Analyst (BCaBA) or RBT receiving supervision?				

CASE 98: VARIED EXPERTISE

Shanice is a BCBA as well as a Speech-Language Pathologist (SLP). Within her current employment at an ABA agency, she is often asked to provide services and strategies using either or both of her areas of expertise.

Applicable Ethics Code(s):				
Rationale for Chosen Code(s):				
Code Violation?	Yes	No	Need More Information	If Situation Continues
Antecedent Factors Contributing to Scenario:				
Preventative Strategies:				
Ethical Course of Action:				
Future Risk Factors to Keep in Mind:				
Discussion Questions:				
Would Shanice's responsibility to the Code be different if she was hired by her company because of her SLP expertise?				

CASE 99: RESPONDING TO REVIEWS

Matilda is a BCBA working at an ABA agency. While searching the Internet, she came across her company's profile on a popular review website. As she scrolled through the posts, she noticed a fairly scathing review written by Cynthia, the parent of Cruz, one of the learners Matilda supervises. Along with Matilda, two of Cruz's direct care staff members were specifically mentioned by their first names in the review. On several occasions, Matilda has met with Cynthia to discuss Cruz's intervention plan, her recommendations, and Cruz's progress. During these meetings, she has never been given the impression that Cynthia was upset or had questions. Matilda responded to the review by posting on the website that she has "done everything I could to help Cruz, and if you did not make him miss so many sessions and followed through with more of my recommendations, maybe he would be doing better."

Applicable Ethics Code(s)				
Rationale for Chosen Code(s):				
Code Violation?	Yes	No	Need More Information	If Situation Continues
Antecedent Factors Contributing to Scenario:				
Preventative Strategies:				
Ethical Course of Action:				
Future Risk Factors to Keep in Mind:				
Discussion Questions:				
Are there still ethical challenges related to the Code if Matilda responded on the review website to Cynthia's comments by saying, "I am sorry to hear about your concerns and frustrations. I hope that we can talk about this in more detail as soon as possible or at Cruz's next team meeting."?				

CASE 100: GOOD INTENTIONS

Rhys has a son who has been diagnosed with ASD and has been receiving ABA services. Seeing the progress his son has made and knowing the lack of services available to many similar children, Rhys hired several BCBAs and RBTs and began his own ABA agency. The website promoting Rhys's company includes information about ABA, provides the background and history of Rhys and his son's involvement in ABA services, and includes pictures and quotes from other current clients describing their experience working with Rhys's agency.

Applicable Ethics Code(s):				
Rationale for Chosen Code(s):				
Code Violation?	Yes	No	Need More Information	If Situation Continues
Antecedent Factors Contributing to Scenario:				
Preventative Strategies:				
Ethical Course of Action:				
Future Risk Factors to Keep in Mind:				
Discussion Questions:				
What is Rhys's obligation to the Code?				
What, if any, obligation do the BCBAs and RBTs working for Rhys's company have in addressing this scenario?				

CASE 101: #HASHTAG

Megan loves her job as an RBT and is passionate about working with her cases. One of the learners, Dante, to whom she has been providing services for a little over a year, was just awarded "Student of the Month" from his school. When Megan arrived for her session, Dante raced to his backpack to show Megan his certificate. They were both extremely excited and proud. To commemorate the accomplishment, Megan took a selfie with Dante holding the award and posted it to her social media account with the caption, "So proud of this kiddo. He has worked so hard. Love my job! #ABARULES #amazingkiddo #studentofthemonth."

Applicable Ethics Code(s):				
Rationale for Chosen Code(s):				
Code Violation?	Yes	No	Need More Information	If Situation Continues
Antecedent Factors Contributing to Scenario:				
Preventative Strategies:				
Ethical Course of Action:				
Future Risk Factors to Keep in Mind:				
Discussion Questions:				
What thoughts might you have if Dante's mother took the picture of Dante and Megan and posted it to her own social media account?				

CASE 102: INTERNET TROLL

Jin is a BCBA and is a member of several ABA groups on Facebook. He recently came across a group moderated by Kris, who provided her full name and stated that she is a BCBA. Kris describes the Facebook group as the "water cooler" for BCBAs looking to vent about their jobs and their clients. Scrolling through the group, Jin noticed that Kris posts a lot about her frustration with parents and teachers. Though Kris does not specifically identify the names of the learners to whom she provides services, she often calls them by derogatory names. Jin noticed that a few others who identify themselves as BCBAs also posted links on the page and made similar negative comments about their cases.

Applicable Ethics Code(s):				
Rationale for Chosen Code(s):				
Code Violation?	Yes	No	Need More Information	If Situation Continues
Antecedent Factors Contributing to Scenario:				
Preventative Strategies:				
Ethical Course of Action:				
Future Risk Factors to Keep in Mind:				
Discussion Questions:				
Do you think Jin's obligations would be met if he were to contact Kris directly to discuss his concerns about the group if Kris were to edit the previous posts to remove any potentially identifying information or derogatory statements? What are Kris's ethical responsibilities?				

Thomas, Cynthia, and Craig are all BCBAs working for an ABA agency. Thomas and Cynthia are both extremely knowledgeable in ABA and charismatic and have excellent business acumen. They developed and ran all the staff trainings for the agency and independently led study groups for the staff who were planning to take the BCBA exam. They have decided to start their own company focusing on exam preparation and study materials and have asked Craig to review their promotional materials. In an effort to make their company stand out from other exam preparation companies, Thomas and Cynthia have named their company "BCBA Exam Success." Their website has the Behavior Analyst Certification Board (BACB) logo on the front page and several testimonials promoting their company. Craig recognizes the comments as staff who have participated in Thomas's and Cynthia's study groups and trainings but have not actually used the "BCBA Exam Success" product.

Applicable Ethics Code(s):				
Rationale for Chosen Code(s):				
Code Violation?	Yes	No	Need More Information	If Situation Continues
Antecedent Factors Contributing to Scenario:				
Preventative Strategies:				
Ethical Course of Action:				
Future Risk Factors to Keep in Mind:				
Discussion Questions:				
How might your responses change if Thomas and Cynthia provided their exam preparation services free of charge?				

Malcolm is a BCBA in private practice. He received a phone call from a representative stating they are with the "Top 10 BCBAs" publication. Malcolm was informed that for a monthly fee, his name and contact information would be added to the list of top 10 BCBAs, and he would be able to advertise himself as one of the "Top 10 BCBAs."

Applicable Ethics Code(s):				
Rationale for Chosen Code(s):				
Code Violation?	Yes	No	Need More Information	If Situation Continues
Antecedent Factors Contributing to Scenario:				
Preventative Strategies:				
Ethical Course of Action:				
Future Risk Factors to Keep in Mind:				
Discussion Questions:				
How would you suggest Malcolm respond to the company representative?				

Chapter 10

Section 6: Responsibility in Research

Standards related to the research practices of behavior analysts developed in response to the morally question-able treatment of research participants. Most ethical issues involving research will not only be addressed within the Code but will also be overseen by Institutional Review Boards (IRBs) and state and federal laws. The ethical implications of research conducted by behavior analysts do not only impact those individuals or organizations who are the direct participants of the research procedure. Rather, when behavior-analytic studies are conducted, there is a connection to those individuals acting as research assistants, students, coauthors, and ultimately the community that accesses the research findings once published. As a result, behavior-analytic research has the potential to impact and influence a vast audience (Bailey & Burch, 2016).

A Workbook of Ethical Case Scenarios in Applied Behavior Analysis, Second Edition. https://doi.org/10.1016/B978-0-323-98813-1.00007-4

CASE 105: CRUNCH THE NUMBERS

After utilizing a particular behavior reduction strategy for several learners, Sasha, a Board Certified Behavior Analyst (BCBA), would like to share her results and findings with a wider audience. She receives permission from several learners to start implementing the behavioral strategy and record the data for potential publication or to present at local Applied Behavior Analysis (ABA) conferences. Sasha is really excited to get started. Though she has never formally conducted a research study before, she is confident in her capabilities of performing the strategy and reviewing the data and results.

Applicable Ethics Code(s):				
Rationale for Chosen Code(s):				
Code Violation?	Yes	No	Need More Information	If Situation Continues
Antecedent Factors Contributing to Scenario:				
Preventative Strategies:				
Ethical Course of Action:				
Future Risk Factors to Keep in Mind:				
Discussion Questions:				
What (if any) ethical codes might apply if Sasha implemented the strategy without the intent of conducting research or for the purpose of publication?				
Would there continue to be any ethical concerns if Sasha was also working with another behavior analyst who could provide guidance throughout the research process?				

CASE 106: UNDUE INFLUENCE

Jiang is a BCBA with a primary focus on researching the effects of various intervention strategies on the reduction of challenging behavior. She received a large grant from a pharmaceutical company to review the effects of a well-regarded function-based intervention strategy in the reduction of challenging behavior for young adults prescribed a particular medication, as compared with those that are not prescribed any medication. Along with the details of her grant, Jiang received a message from the pharmaceutical company reminding her that, "This is an expensive study with a lot riding on this medication. We trust you will do the right thing for the company."

Applicable Ethics Code(s):				
Rationale for Chosen Code(s):				
Code Violation?	Yes	No	Need More Information	If Situation Continues
Antecedent Factors Contributing to Scenario:				
Preventative Strategies:				
Ethical Course of Action:				
Future Risk Factors to Keep in Mind:				
Discussion Questions:				
How might Jiang's responsibility change if she did not receive the message from the company sponsoring the research?				

CASE 107: ET AL

Suni is a doctoral-level Board Certified Behavior Analyst (BCBA-D) and thesis advisor to Nataly, a student in an ABA Master's program. After completing her thesis, Suni suggested Nataly work with her to prepare her paper to submit for potential publication. The two collaborated in editing the manuscript and adding a more comprehensive discussion section. Suni included herself as the first author, as she holds a higher degree, was the advisor on the project, and completed the journal submission process.

Applicable Ethics Code(s):				
Rationale for Chosen Code(s):				
Code Violation?	Yes	No	Need More Information	If Situation Continues
Antecedent Factors Contributing to Scenario:				
Preventative Strategies:				
Ethical Course of Action:				
Future Risk Factors to Keep in Mind:				

Complex Scenarios Involving Multiple Sections of the Code

Perhaps the greatest concern related to a violation of the Code is the harm that may be caused toward those involved, particularly the most vulnerable. Even the most straightforward, singular ethical transgression could have lasting impact and repercussions. The complexity of an ethical scenario does not necessarily directly translate to greater risk. However, it is important when studying ethics in applied behavior analysis (ABA) to avoid considering a violation as though it occurs within a vacuum by compartmentalizing each area of the Code and responding systematically as though only a specific infraction has occurred before moving onto the next relevant section.

Of the alleged ethics notices submitted to the Behavior Analyst Certification Board (BACB) in 2016 and 2017, approximately 34% contained only one actionable violation, 32% contained two, 22% contained three, 9% contained four, and approximately 4% contained five or more actionable violations. While notices containing only one actionable violation were comparatively the largest subgroup, the majority of notices that were ultimately found to result in an actionable violation (approximately 67%) contained two or more violations of the Code (BACB, 2018).

The factors that influence the occurrence of an ethics violation are likely unique and dependent on particular situational variables. As violations increase in complexity, the identification of the path that led to the ethical challenge is likely significantly more convoluted. Similarly, as an ethical dilemma becomes more multifaceted, the response will likely be more involved and intricate. The final chapter of this workbook includes several ethically challenging scenarios wherein one section of the Code may not necessarily be considered the primary concern. Instead, various aspects of the Code may be applicable and necessary for review and consideration.

CASE 108: NO SHOW, OH NO!

Noah is a Board Certified Behavior Analyst (BCBA) supervising Anita's program within a private elementary school setting. One day he received a call from the school asking how Harriet, a Registered Behavior Technician (RBT) who provides direct behavioral intervention, grounded in ABA to Anita, is feeling. After asking for more details related to the school's concern, Noah came to find out that Harriet had not attended any of her shifts with Anita at the school for the last several weeks (aside from the days when Noah attended to observe). The school did not seem bothered that Harriet was absent from her shifts with Anita, but rather, was more concerned with her health. Looking at the past billing and attendance records for Anita, it appears that Harriet has continued to sign in and out as if she were conducting behavioral intervention sessions with Anita at the school. As a result, Anita's insurance company has already been billed for the sessions as if the RBT had provided services. No one else at the ABA agency was aware that Harriet did not provide services at the school. Thus, no alternative coverage was provided. Anita had been provided services by Noah's agency during shifts covered by the agency's other staff members but was only supported by the general school staff during shifts that were supposed to be conducted by Harriet.

Applicable Ethics Code(s):				
Rationale for Chosen Code(s):				
Code Violation?	Yes	No	Need More Information	If Situation Continues
Antecedent Factors Contributing to Scenario:				
Preventative Strategies:				
Ethical Course of Action:				
Future Risk Factors to Keep in Mind:				
Discussion Questions:				
How might Noah or Harriet's ethical responsibility change if Anita engaged in more dangerous challenging behavior such as aggression or elopement?				
Does Noah have a responsibility to inform Anita's parents of Harriet's missed sessions?				

CASE 109: SPLITTING UP IS HARD TO DO

Kiana is a BCBA supervising a small team of RBTs working with a young learner with autism spectrum disorder (ASD). Kiana has just learned that the parents of the learner have recently filed for divorce. With the permission of the learner's mother, Kiana is discussing the divorce with the team to address any program changes or anticipated challenges. Upon disclosing the news with her team, Kiana found that her team was not surprised by the parents' decision. One staff member said, "Finally! Those two are constantly fighting during sessions. They are on their best behavior when you come to supervise, but it's usually hard to get anything done during our sessions. Half of the time I feel like we are referees." Another staff member mentioned that he often holds his sessions outside in the backyard to avoid hearing the parents' arguments. A third staff member stated that he was already aware of the divorce because the learner's mother asked if he would be willing to write a letter (to use as evidence in the upcoming divorce proceedings) stating that he believes it would be inappropriate for the father to hold dual custody of the learner due to being unsupportive of ABA and exhibiting a parenting style that is not conducive to caring for a child diagnosed with ASD. The staff member has been avoiding writing the letter but feels obligated since the mother is always the one who is home during his sessions.

Applicable Ethics Code(s):				
Rationale for Chosen Code(s):				
Code Violation?	Yes	No	Need More Information	If Situation Continues
Antecedent Factors Contributing to Scenario:				
Preventative Strategies:				
Ethical Course of Action:				
Future Risk Factors to Keep in Mind:				
Discussion Questions:				
Should Kiana's response change if she had learned of the team's challenges earlier?				

CASE 110: ACADEMIC ADVOCACY

Lamar is a BCBA who has been supervising ABA services for Tyson in the home and school settings for the past 2 years. Recently, Tyson was transferred from a public to a private school that reportedly specializes in providing education to children with developmental disabilities (DD). Though Tyson has changed schools, Lamar and his agency remain contracted to provide ABA services in the new location. At the initial school meeting, Lamar learns that the school uses intervention procedures that would not be considered behavioral in nature and have questionable research-backing. The school staff do not seem happy that the parents advocated for continued ABA services and have repeatedly stated that they do not think ABA is a good match for this student in this environment. The school administration has stated that in order for Lamar's agency to continue services, they expect Lamar to conform to the school's intervention methodologies, rather than employing strategies and procedures based in ABA. Lamar contacted his funding source to discuss the potential need to find alternative services, and the representative encouraged Lamar to have his team work within the parameters set by the school.

Applicable Ethics Code(s):				
Rationale for Chosen Code(s):				
Code Violation?	Yes	No	Need More Information	If Situation Continues
Antecedent Factors Contributing to Scenario:				
Preventative Strategies:				
Ethical Course of Action:				
Future Risk Factors to Keep in Mind:				
Discussion Questions:				
How might Lamar address the school's concerns and opinions?				

CASE 111: SOMETHING'S IN THE AIR

Ava is an RBT who provides direct intervention to an adult, Rod, diagnosed with a DD. When she arrived at Rod's house, Rod's mother (whom Rod lives with) asked Ava to integrate scented sprays within sessions. One spray is meant to be used when Rod is particularly "rowdy" to calm him down, and the other is an "alerting spray" when he needs to "perk up a bit." The sprays are nontoxic, mostly smelling of lavender for the calming spray and citrus for the alerting spray. Rod's mother told Ava that the other RBT who had sessions earlier in the week has already started using the sprays. Rod's mother is particularly excited about using the sprays because she has heard great results from another parent of a learner that attends Rod's day program. Ava is unsure whether the BCBA supervising the case is aware of the use of the scented sprays.

Applicable Ethics Code(s):				
Rationale for Chosen Code(s):				
Code Violation?	Yes	No	Need More Information	If Situation Continues
Antecedent Factors Contributing to Scenario:				
Preventative Strategies:				
Ethical Course of Action:				
Future Risk Factors to Keep in Mind:				
Discussion Questions:				
How might your response to the scenario differ if the other RBT working with Rod had not already started using the scented sprays within sessions?				
How might your response differ if you discovered that the scents are highly preferred by Rod?				

CASE 112: BURY THE LEAD

Annabelle is a BCBA supervising the ABA services of an adolescent whose services are funded through the school district. Based on some questions regarding the student's progress, the school has audited Annabelle's agency's records related to the services provided. Annabelle and her staff are compiling available records related to the intervention for the student. As they are organizing the data, Annabelle notices that several data sheets are missing for days when services were said to have been provided, and an assessment that was supposed to have been completed within the previous month has not yet been initiated. Annabelle has another day to provide all the paperwork, which gives her enough time to complete the assessment and her report. Since she only missed the assessment deadline expectation by a month and she has a record of the student's progress during that time period, she dates the report as having been previously completed within the assigned timeframe. Annabelle also writes a letter in her records provided to the school district apologizing for the missing datasheets. She notes in the letter that though services were completed on the days listed and have been integrated into the student's graphs, she is unable to locate the corresponding raw data records.

Applicable Ethics Code(s):				
Rationale for Chosen Code(s):				
Code Violation?	Yes	No	Need More Information	If Situation Continues
Antecedent Factors Contributing to Scenario:				
Preventative Strategies:				
Ethical Course of Action:				
Future Risk Factors to Keep in Mind:				
Discussion Questions:				
Should Annabelle have done anything differently?				

Bennett is a BCBA who oversees a group program for teens who have been diagnosed with ASD. Dylan, a member of the group, was born female and identified as male. Dylan has indicated a preference for using "they/them" pronouns. All records and available paperwork for Dylan list Dylan's gender as female and include Dylan's birthname, Dara. Since greetings and other social skills are practiced within the group, Bennett asks Dylan to use their birth name and "she/her" pronouns to assist the other members. Whenever Dylan uses their chosen name, Bennett "corrects" Dylan, and if another member of the group greets Dylan using the name "Dara," the member is praised by Bennett.

Applicable Ethics Code(s):				
Rationale for Chosen Code(s):				
Code Violation?	Yes	No	Need More Information	If Situation Continues
Antecedent Factors Contributing to Scenario:				
Preventative Strategies:				
Ethical Course of Action:				
Future Risk Factors to Keep in Mind:				

CASE 114: MY WAY OR THE HIGHWAY

Samar is a BCBA who provides services to Deon, a 12-year-old male diagnosed with intellectual disability. Samar has found that Deon's family does not seem to implement any of his recommendations. For example, Samar's direct care staff have reported that Deon is often in diapers at the start of his sessions, despite the recommendation to only use underwear in support of Deon's toilet training program. In addition, the staff regularly find Deon playing on his tablet when they arrive for sessions, despite the parents initially agreeing to the tablet being a contingent reinforcer for correct responding during intervention sessions. Given these challenges, Samar has informed the parents that his agency will no longer provide ABA services, and he has offered several recommended referrals to other agencies.

Applicable Ethics Code(s):				
Rationale for Chosen Code(s):				
Code Violation?	Yes	No	Need More Information	If Situation Continues
Antecedent Factors Contributing to Scenario:				
Preventative Strategies:				
Ethical Course of Action:				
Future Risk Factors to Keep in Mind:				
Discussion Questions:				
How might you suggest Samar's response change if Deon's family promises to make the suggested changes to support the program?				
What if Deon's family had already made this promise several times?				

144 11. Complex Scenarios Involving Multiple Sections of the Code

CASE 115: SIGN ON THE DOTTED LINE

Jada, a BCBA, supervises a large caseload with the support of Devon, a Board Certified Assistant Behavior Analyst (BCaBA). The two have been working together for over a year and have a good sense of each other's writing style and clinical decision-making. Devon often writes the behavior intervention plans and progress reports for the learners Jada supervises, and Jada signs the reports before submitting them to the requesting party.

Applicable Ethics Code(s):				
Rationale for Chosen Code(s):				
Code Violation?	Yes	No	Need More Information	If Situation Continues
Antecedent Factors Contributing to Scenario:				
Preventative Strategies:				
Ethical Course of Action:				
Future Risk Factors to Keep in Mind:				

CASE 116: LOST IN TRANSLATION

Riley is an RBT working with Heon Woo within the home setting. Heon Woo's parents are out of the house at work, and his grandmother, who does not speak English, is the only adult home during all of Riley's sessions. As a result, Riley and her staff are not able to address any concerns that may arise with Heon Woo's grandmother. Following each session, Riley or her team will leave a note with some general updates for Heon Woo's parents to read, but the team rarely has the opportunity to discuss Heon Woo's progress with the parents due to the scheduling conflicts.

Applicable Ethics Code(s):				
Rationale for Chosen Code(s):				
Code Violation?	Yes	No	Need More Information	If Situation Continues
Antecedent Factors Contributing to Scenario:				
Preventative Strategies:				
Ethical Course of Action:				
Future Risk Factors to Keep in Mind:				

CASE 117: MAD SCIENTIST

Marco is accruing supervised experience hours toward his BCBA exam under the direction of Dr. Stargyen at a local university. In addition to clinical and administrative services, Marco works as Dr. Stargyen's research assistant. Most of the participants within Dr. Stargyen's studies attend a specialized treatment clinic within the university. Dr. Stargyen is initiating a new study and has directed Marco to begin compiling baseline data with the selected participants. At a treatment team meeting for one of the participants, attended by the parents, Marco mentioned his data collection process for the study. The parents were very upset as they had no idea their son was involved in research while attending the treatment clinic. Marco was asked to meet with Dr. Stargyen later that day who stated that all the parents should know that their children will be involved in some type of research because they attend a specialized clinic at the university. Marco was told that if he speaks with a parent again about the research he can "find another supervisor" and that Dr. Stargyen would not be signing off on the supervision hours Marco completed this month.

Applicable Ethics Code(s):				
Rationale for Chosen Code(s):				
Code Violation?	Yes	No	Need More Information	If Situation Continues
Antecedent Factors Contributing to Scenario:				
Preventative Strategies:				
Ethical Course of Action:				
Future Risk Factors to Keep in Mind:				
Discussion Questions:				
Was Marco out of place discussing the research protocol with the parents of the learners who attend the university clinic?				

Valentina is a BCBA and a member of several ABA-themed and ASD-themed Facebook groups. Often, people practicing behavior analysis or parents write into the groups either sharing their experiences or asking for thoughts and advice. Valentina noticed a post from Christie, a mother asking for some advice about her 2-year-old son. Christie explained that her son was displaying some "odd" behaviors, but she had not yet taken him for an evaluation or to her pediatrician. Several other members of the group, who identified themselves as BCBAs, commented on the post. Some shamed Christie for not already having a diagnosis or enrolling her son in ABA services, others told Christie that her son was "definitely autistic," and others provided her with specific interventions to reduce the mentioned challenging behaviors.

Applicable Ethics Code(s):				
Rationale for Chosen Code(s):				
Code Violation?	Yes	No	Need More Information	If Situation Continues
Antecedent Factors Contributing to Scenario:				
Preventative Strategies:				
Ethical Course of Action:				
Future Risk Factors to Keep in Mind:				

CASE 119: WEAR MANY HATS

Halloway Behavioral Services is a moderately sized ABA agency with three offices and several BCBAs on staff. Each month, the BCBAs meet to hold clinical grand rounds where staff have the opportunity to discuss cases and provide peer support. At each meeting, one BCBA is asked to present a case by reviewing the current intervention plan and relevant assessments. During his turn to present, Rohan, who is a Licensed Clinical Social Worker in addition to a BCBA, gave a report for one of his current cases who is a young adolescent diagnosed with a DD. The learner is funded for 25 hours per week of one-to-one ABA-based intervention and 5 hours per month of supervision by a BCBA. Rohan discussed the learner's various lessons and goals and also mentioned as part of his allotted supervision hours that he meets with the learner directly for talk-based individual therapy sessions. Rohan demonstrated data supporting an increase in communication, as well as a decrease in targeted challenging behavior coinciding with his initiation of individual therapy.

Applicable Ethics Code(s):				
Rationale for Chosen Code(s):				
Code Violation?	Yes	No	Need More Information	If Situation Continues
Antecedent Factors Contributing to Scenario:				
Preventative Strategies:				
Ethical Course of Action:				
Future Risk Factors to Keep in Mind:				
Discussion Questions:				
As a BCBA, is Rohan able to provide clinical services as a social worker?				

CASE 120: NEED FOR CONCERN?

Andres is a BCaBA providing services to Lilo within the home and clinic settings. When providing services for Lilo at his home, Andres consistently notices several new empty bottles of alcohol. Andres has never actually observed Lilo's mother drinking alcohol. However, on several occasions, when Lilo's mother arrived to pick up Lilo from the clinic, Andres believed he may have smelled alcohol on Lilo's mother's breath. Today, when Lilo was picked up by his mother, in addition to the smell of alcohol, Andres noticed Lilo's mother slurring her words and stumbling when walking from her car.

Applicable Ethics Code(s):				
Rationale for Chosen Code(s):				
Code Violation?	Yes	No	Need More Information	If Situation Continues
Antecedent Factors Contributing to Scenario:				
Preventative Strategies:				
Ethical Course of Action:				
Future Risk Factors to Keep in Mind:				

CASE 121: GLITCH

Octavia, a Board Certified Behavior Analyst—Doctoral (BDBA-D), has recently transitioned from a paper-and-pencil data collection method to a computer-based system. Once the data are recorded, the system integrates the information, develops graphs and comparative data, and self-generates written reports that can be submitted to parents, schools, and funding organizations. Along with not having to carry around a large binder for each learner, the new system saves Octavia time reviewing data and writing reports. Octavia has already submitted a number of progress reports to funding organizations using the computer-based system but has been asked to discuss several cases with the funding source as information contained within the reports appears to be missing or inaccurate.

Applicable Ethics Code(s):				
Rationale for Chosen Code(s):				
Code Violation?	Yes	No	Need More Information	If Situation Continues
Antecedent Factors Contributing to Scenario:				
Preventative Strategies:				
Ethical Course of Action:				
Future Risk Factors to Keep in Mind:				
Discussion Questions:				
What would be an ethically appropriate way for Octavia to use the electronic data collection system?				
What step in this process of ethically appropriate use of an electronic data collection system has Octavia likely left out?				

CASE 122: BEHIND CLOSED DOORS

Mateo is a BCBA providing in-home services to families. One of his cases, Jackson, is a 19-year-old male diagnosed with intellectual disability and living in his parents' home. Jackson has recently begun to engage in masturbation. He typically engages in this behavior when in his bedroom or bathroom, but the door is often open. During a team meeting, Jackson's parents express their concern with this behavior and ask Mateo to implement an intervention with the goal being to stop Jackson from engaging in masturbation altogether. To eliminate the behavior, they suggest Mateo develop a plan where Jackson will be reprimanded and lose access to his computer whenever he engages in masturbation. Mateo has not discussed the behavior with Jackson directly. When asked if Jackson's parents have addressed any concerns with Jackson, they responded, "this isn't something we talk about."

Applicable Ethics Code(s):				
Rationale for Chosen Code(s):				
Code Violation?	Yes	No	Need More Information	If Situation Continues
Antecedent Factors Contributing to Scenario:				
Preventative Strategies:				
Ethical Course of Action:				
Future Risk Factors to Keep in Mind:				
Discussion Questions:				
How would you suggest Mateo ethically navigate the concerns of Jackson's parents, as well as Jackson's preferences?				

CASE 123: ADAPT AND ADJUST

Max is a BCBA supervising ABA services for Theo, who experiences regular grand mal and petit mal seizures. Max and his staff have been trained to identify when a seizure has occurred, ensure Theo's safety to the best of their ability, and seek support when necessary. After more significant seizure activity, Theo is often very lethargic for several days and has difficulty participating in ABA sessions. On occasion, he has demonstrated regression following a seizure and may no longer perform skills that were previously considered mastered. Max has not developed a plan for addressing session expectations for the days following a more severe seizure and has not yet established a strategy for accurately recording data for skills that may no longer be consistently performed after a seizure has occurred. As a result, Max and his staff may not reintroduce previously mastered targets into Theo's skill acquisition programming.

Applicable Ethics Code(s):				
Rationale for Chosen Code(s):				
Code Violation?	Yes	No	Need More Information	If Situation Continues
Antecedent Factors Contributing to Scenario:				
Preventative Strategies:				
Ethical Course of Action:				
Future Risk Factors to Keep in Mind:				
Discussion Questions:				
What clinical or ethical challenges may occur if Max and his team were to continue to follow their current practices in relation to Theo's programming and data collection?				

Appendix A: Ethics Code for Behavior Analysts

The Ethics Code for Behavior Analysts (Code) replaces the Professional and Ethical Compliance Code for Behavior Analysts (2014). All BCBA and BCaBA applicants and certifiants are required to adhere to the Code effective January 1, 2022.

TABLE OF CONTENTS

SECTION 2—RESPONSIBILITY IN PRACTICE

SECTION 3—RESPONSIBILITY TO CLIENTS AND STAKEHOLDERS   167

SECTION 4—RESPONSIBILITY TO SUPERVISEES AND TRAINEES   169

INTRODUCTION

As a diverse group of professionals who work in a variety of practice areas, behavior analysts deliver applied behavior analysis (ABA) services to positively impact lives. The Behavior Analyst Certification Board® (BACB®) exists to meet the credentialing needs of these professionals and relevant stakeholders (e.g., licensure boards, funders) while protecting ABA consumers by establishing, disseminating, and managing professional standards. The BACB facilitates ethical behavior in the profession through its certification eligibility and maintenance requirements, by issuing the ethics standards described in this document, and by operating a system for addressing professional misconduct.

The Ethics Code for Behavior Analysts (Code) guides the professional activities of behavior analysts over whom the BACB has jurisdiction (see *Scope of the Code* below). The Code also provides a means for behavior analysts to evaluate their own behavior and for others to assess whether a behavior analyst has violated their ethical obligations. An **introduction** section describes the scope and application of the Code, its core principles, and considerations for ethical decision making. The core principles are foundational concepts that should guide all aspects of a behavior analyst's work. The introduction is followed by a **glossary** that includes definitions of technical terms used in the Code. The final section includes the **ethics standards,** which are informed by the core principles. The standards are organized into six sections: 1) Responsibility as a Professional, 2) Responsibility in Practice, 3) Responsibility to Clients and Stakeholders, 4) Responsibility to Supervisees and Trainees, 5) Responsibility in Public Statements, and 6) Responsibility in Research.

SCOPE OF THE CODE

The Code applies to all individuals who hold Board Certified Behavior Analyst® (BCBA®) or Board Certified Assistant Behavior Analyst® (BCaBA®) certification and all individuals who have completed an application for BCBA or BCaBA certification. For the sake of efficiency, the term "behavior analyst" is used throughout this document to refer to those who must act in accordance with the Code. The BACB does not have separate jurisdiction over organizations or corporations.

The Code applies to behavior analysts in all of their professional activities, including direct service delivery, consultation, supervision, training, management, editorial and peer-review activities, research, and any other activity within the ABA profession. The Code applies to behavior analysts' professional activities across settings and delivery modes (e.g., in person; in writing; via phone, email, text message, video conferencing). Application of the Code does not extend to behavior analysts' personal behavior unless it is determined that the behavior clearly poses a potential risk to the health and safety of clients, stakeholders, supervisees, or trainees.

Specific terms are defined in the **Glossary** section; however, two definitions are provided here because they are frequently used in the Core Principles section.

Client: The direct recipient of the behavior analyst's services. At various times during service provision, one or more stakeholders may simultaneously meet the definition of client (e.g., the point at which they receive direct training or consultation). In some contexts, the client might be a group of individuals (e.g., with organizational behavior management services).

Stakeholder: An individual, other than the client, who is impacted by and invested in the behavior analyst's services (e.g., parent, caregiver, relative, legally authorized representative, collaborator, employer, agency or institutional representative, licensure board, funder, third-party contractor for services).

CORE PRINCIPLES

Four foundational principles, which all behavior analysts should strive to embody, serve as the framework for the ethics standards. Behavior analysts should use these principles to interpret and apply the standards in the Code. The four core principles are that behavior analysts should: benefit others; treat others with compassion, dignity, and respect; behave with integrity; and ensure their own competence.

1. **Benefit Others.** Behavior analysts work to maximize benefits and do no harm by:
   - Protecting the welfare and rights of clients above all others
   - Protecting the welfare and rights of other individuals with whom they interact in a professional capacity
   - Focusing on the short- and long-term effects of their professional activities
   - Actively identifying and addressing the potential negative impacts of their own physical and mental health on their professional activities
   - Actively identifying potential and actual conflicts of interest and working to resolve them in a manner that avoids or minimizes harm
   - Actively identifying and addressing factors (e.g., personal, financial, institutional, political, religious, cultural) that might lead to conflicts of interest, misuse of their position, or negative impacts on their professional activities
   - Effectively and respectfully collaborating with others in the best interest of those with whom they work and always placing clients' interests first

2. **Treat Others with Compassion, Dignity, and Respect.** Behavior analysts behave toward others with compassion, dignity, and respect by:
   - Treating others equitably, regardless of factors such as age, disability, ethnicity, gender expression/identity, immigration status, marital/relationship status, national origin, race, religion, sexual orientation, socioeconomic status, or any other basis proscribed by law
   - Respecting others' privacy and confidentiality
   - Respecting and actively promoting clients' self-determination to the best of their abilities, particularly when providing services to vulnerable populations
   - Acknowledging that personal choice in service delivery is important by providing clients and stakeholders with needed information to make informed choices about services

3. **Behave with Integrity.** Behavior analysts fulfill responsibilities to their scientific and professional communities, to society in general, and to the communities they serve by:
   - Behaving in an honest and trustworthy manner
   - Not misrepresenting themselves, misrepresenting their work or others' work, or engaging in fraud
   - Following through on obligations
   - Holding themselves accountable for their work and the work of their supervisees and trainees, and correcting errors in a timely manner
   - Being knowledgeable about and upholding BACB and other regulatory requirements
   - Actively working to create professional environments that uphold the core principles and standards of the Code
   - Respectfully educating others about the ethics requirements of behavior analysts and the mechanisms for addressing professional misconduct

4. Ensure their Competence. Behavior analysts ensure their competence by:
- Remaining within the profession's scope of practice
- Remaining current and increasing their knowledge of best practices and advances in ABA and participating in professional development activities
- Remaining knowledgeable and current about interventions (including pseudoscience)
- that may exist in their practice areas and pose a risk of harm to clients
- Being aware of, working within, and continually evaluating the boundaries of their competence
- Working to continually increase their knowledge and skills related to cultural responsiveness and service delivery to diverse groups

APPLICATION OF THE CODE

Behavior analysts are expected to be knowledgeable about and comply with the Code and **Code-Enforcement Procedures**. Lack of awareness or misunderstanding of an ethics standard is not a defense against an alleged ethics violation. When appropriate, behavior analysts should inform others about the Code and Code-Enforcement Procedures and create conditions that foster adherence to the Code. When addressing potential code violations by themselves or others, behavior analysts document the steps taken and the resulting outcomes. Behavior analysts should address concerns about the professional misconduct of others directly with them when, after assessing the situation, it seems possible that doing so will resolve the issue and not place the behavior analyst or others at undue risk.

The BACB recognizes that behavior analysts may have different professional roles. As such, behavior analysts are required to comply with all applicable laws, licensure requirements, codes of conduct/ethics, reporting requirements (e.g., mandated reporting, reporting to funding sources or licensure board, self-reporting to the BACB, reporting instances of misrepresentation by others), and professional practice requirements related to their various roles. In some instances, behavior analysts may need to report serious concerns to relevant authorities or agencies that can provide more immediate relief or protection before reporting to the BACB (e.g., criminal activity or behavior that places clients or others at risk for direct and immediate harm should immediately be reported to the relevant authorities before reporting to the BACB or a licensure board).

The standards included in the Code are not meant to be exhaustive, as it is impossible to predict every situation that might constitute an ethics violation. Therefore, the absence of a particular behavior or type of conduct from the Code standards does not indicate that such behavior or conduct is ethical or unethical. When interpreting and applying a standard, it is critical to attend to its specific wording and function, as well as the core principles. Additionally, standards must be applied to a situation using a functional, contextualized approach that accounts for factors relevant to that situation, such as variables related to diversity (e.g., age, disability, ethnicity, gender expression/identity, immigration status, marital/relationship status, national origin, race, religion, sexual orientation, socioeconomic status) and possible imbalances in power. In all instances of interpreting and applying the Code, behavior analysts should put compliance with the law and clients' interests first by actively working to maximize desired outcomes and minimize risk.

Ethical decision making. Behavior analysts will likely encounter complex and multifaceted ethical dilemmas. When faced with such a dilemma, behavior analysts should identify problems and solutions with care and deliberation. In resolving an ethical dilemma, behavior analysts should follow the spirit and letter of the Code's core principles and specific standards. Behavior analysts should address ethical dilemmas through a structured decision-making process that considers the full context of the situation and the function of relevant ethics standards. Although no single ethical decision-making process will be equally effective in all situations, the process below illustrates a systematic approach behavior analysts can take to document and address potential ethical concerns.

Throughout all of the following steps, document information that may be essential to decision making or for communicating the steps taken and outcomes (e.g., to the BACB, licensure boards, or other governing agencies). For example, consider documenting: dates, times, locations, and relevant individuals; summaries of observations, meetings, or information reported by others. Take care to protect confidentiality in the preparation and storage of all documentation.

---

1. Clearly define the issue and consider potential risk of harm to relevant individuals.
2. Identify all relevant individuals.
3. Gather relevant supporting documentation and follow-up on second-hand information to confirm that there is an actual ethical concern.
4. Consider your personal learning history and biases in the context of the relevant individuals.
5. Identify the relevant core principles and Code standards.

6. Consult available resources (e.g., research, decision-making models, trusted colleagues).
7. Develop several possible actions to reduce or remove risk of harm, prioritizing the best interests of clients in accordance with the Code and applicable laws.
8. Critically evaluate each possible action by considering its alignment with the "letter and spirit" of the Code, its potential impact on the client and stakeholders, the likelihood of it immediately resolving the ethical concern, as well as variables such as client preference, social acceptability, degree of restrictiveness, and likelihood of maintenance.
9. Select the action that seems most likely to resolve the specific ethical concern and reduce the likelihood of similar issues arising in the future.
10. Take the selected action in collaboration with relevant individuals affected by the issue and document specific actions taken, agreed-upon next steps, names of relevant individuals, and due dates.
11. Evaluate the outcomes to ensure that the action successfully addressed the issue.

ENFORCEMENT OF THE CODE

The BACB enforces the Code to protect clients and stakeholders, BCBA and BCaBA certificants and applicants, and the ABA profession. Complaints are received and processed according to the processes outlined in the BACB's Code-Enforcement Procedures document.

GLOSSARY

BEHAVIOR ANALYST

An individual who holds BCBA or BCaBA certification or who has submitted a complete application for BCBA or BCaBA certification.

BEHAVIOR-CHANGE INTERVENTION

The full set of behavioral procedures designed to improve the client's wellbeing.

BEHAVIORAL SERVICES

Services that are explicitly based on the principles and procedures of behavior analysis and are designed to change behavior in meaningful ways. These services include, but are not limited to, assessment, behavior-change interventions, training, consultation, managing and supervising others, and delivering continuing education.

CLIENT

The direct recipient of the behavior analyst's services. At various times during service provision, one or more stakeholders may simultaneously meet the definition of client (e.g., the point at which they receive direct training or consultation). In some contexts, the client might be a group of individuals (e.g., with organizational behavior management services).

CLIENTS' RIGHTS

Human rights, legal rights, rights codified within behavior analysis, and organization rules designed to benefit the client.

CONFLICT OF INTEREST

An incompatibility between a behavior analysts' private and professional interests resulting in risk or potential risk to services provided to, or the professional relationship with, a client, stakeholder, supervisee, trainee, or research participant. Conflicts may result in a situation in which personal, financial, or professional considerations have the potential to influence or compromise professional judgment in the delivery of behavioral services, research, consultation, supervision, training, or any other professional activity.

DIGITAL CONTENT

Information that is made available for online consumption, downloading, or distribution through an electronic medium (e.g., television, radio, ebook, website, social media, videogame, application, computer, smart device). Common digital content includes documents, pictures, videos, and audio files.

INFORMED CONSENT

The permission given by an individual with the legal right to consent before participating in services or research, or allowing their information to be used or shared.

> *Service/Research: Providing the opportunity for an individual to give informed consent for services or research involves communicating about and taking appropriate steps to confirm understanding of: 1) the purpose of the services or research; 2) the expected time commitment and procedures involved; 3) the right to decline to participate or withdraw at any time without adverse consequences; 4) potential benefits, risks, discomfort, or adverse effects; 5) any limits to confidentiality or privacy; 6) any incentives for research participation; 7) whom to contact for questions or concerns at any time; and 8) the opportunity to ask questions and receive answers.*
>
> *Information Use/Sharing: Providing the opportunity for an individual to give informed consent to share or use their information involves communicating about: 1) the purpose and intended use; 2) the audience; 3) the expected duration; 4) the right to decline or withdraw consent at any time; 5) potential risks or benefits; 6) any limitations to confidentiality or privacy; 7) whom to contact for questions or concerns at any time; and 8) the opportunity to ask questions and receive answers.*

LEGALLY AUTHORIZED REPRESENTATIVE

Any individual authorized under law to provide consent on behalf of an individual who cannot provide consent to receive services or participate in research.

MULTIPLE RELATIONSHIP

A comingling of two or more of a behavior analyst's roles (e.g., behavioral and personal) with a client, stakeholder, supervisee, trainee, research participant, or someone closely associated with or related to the client.

PUBLIC STATEMENTS

Delivery of information (digital or otherwise) in a public forum for the purpose of either better informing that audience or providing a call-to-action. This includes paid or unpaid advertising, brochures, printed material, directory listings, personal resumes or curriculum vitae, interviews, or comments for use in media (e.g., print, statements in legal proceedings, lectures and public presentations, social media, published materials).

RESEARCH

Any data-based activity, including analysis of preexisting data, designed to generate generalizable knowledge for the discipline. The use of an experimental design does not by itself constitute research.

RESEARCH PARTICIPANT

Any individual participating in a defined research study for whom informed consent has been obtained.

RESEARCH REVIEW COMMITTEE

A group of professionals whose stated purpose is to review research proposals to ensure the ethical treatment of human research participants. This committee might be an official entity of a government or university (e.g., Institutional Review Board, Research Ethics Board), an independent committee within a service organization, or an independent organization created for this purpose.

SCOPE OF COMPETENCE

The professional activities a behavior analyst can consistently perform with proficiency.

SOCIAL MEDIA CHANNEL

A digital platform, either found through a web browser or through an application, where users (individuals and/or businesses) can consume, create, copy, download, share, or comment on posts or advertisements. Both posts and advertisements would be considered digital content.

STAKEHOLDER

An individual, other than the client, who is impacted by and invested in the behavior analyst's services (e.g., parent, caregiver, relative, legally authorized representative, collaborator, employer, agency or institutional representatives, licensure board, funder, third-party contractor for services).

SUPERVISEE

Any individual whose behavioral service delivery is overseen by a behavior analyst within the context of a defined, agreed-upon relationship. Supervisees may include RBTs, BCaBAs, and BCBAs, as well as other professionals carrying out supervised behavioral services.

TESTIMONIAL

Any solicited or unsolicited recommendation, in any form, from a client, stakeholder, supervisee, or trainee affirming the benefits received from a behavior analyst's product or service. From the point at which a behavior analyst asks an individual for a recommendation it is considered solicited.

THIRD PARTY

Any individual, group of individuals, or entity, other than the direct recipient of services, the primary caregiver, the legally authorized representative, or the behavior analyst, who requests and funds services on behalf of a client or group of clients. Some examples include a school district, governmental entity, mental health agency, among others.

TRAINEE

Any individual accruing fieldwork/experience toward fulfilling eligibility requirements for BCaBA or BCBA certification.

WEBSITE

A digital platform found through a web browser where an entity (individual and/or organization) produces and distributes digital content for the consumption of users online. Depending on the functionality, users can consume, create, copy, download, share, or comment on the provided digital content.

Note: Terms defined in the glossary are *italicized* the first time they appear in a standard in each section of the Code.

ETHICS STANDARDS

SECTION 1—RESPONSIBILITY AS A PROFESSIONAL

1.01 *Being Truthful*
Behavior analysts are truthful and arrange the professional environment to promote truthful behavior in others. They do not create professional situations that result in others engaging in behavior that is fraudulent or illegal or that violates the Code. They also provide truthful and accurate information to all required entities (e.g., BACB, licensure boards, funders) and individuals (e.g., clients, stakeholders, supervisees, trainees), and they correct instances of untruthful or inaccurate submissions as soon as they become aware of them.

1.02 Conforming with Legal and Professional Requirements

Behavior analysts follow the law and the requirements of their professional community (e.g., BACB, licensure board).

1.03 Accountability

Behavior analysts are accountable for their actions and professional services and follow through on work commitments. When errors occur or commitments cannot be met, behavior analysts take all appropriate actions to directly address them, first in the best interest of *clients,* and then in the best interest of relevant parties.

1.04 Practicing within a Defined Role

Behavior analysts provide services only after defining and documenting their professional role with relevant parties in writing.

1.05 Practicing within Scope of Competence

Behavior analysts practice only within their identified *scope of competence*. They engage in professional activities in new areas (e.g., populations, procedures) only after accessing and documenting appropriate study, training, supervised experience, consultation, and/or co-treatment from professionals competent in the new area. Otherwise, they refer or transition services to an appropriate professional.

1.06 Maintaining Competence

Behavior analysts actively engage in professional development activities to maintain and further their professional competence. Professional development activities include reading relevant literature; attending conferences and conventions; participating in workshops and other training opportunities; obtaining additional coursework; receiving coaching, consultation, supervision, or mentorship; and obtaining and maintaining appropriate professional credentials.

1.07 Cultural Responsiveness and Diversity

Behavior analysts actively engage in professional development activities to acquire knowledge and skills related to cultural responsiveness and diversity. They evaluate their own biases and ability to address the needs of individuals with diverse needs/backgrounds (e.g., age, disability, ethnicity, gender expression/identity, immigration status, marital/relationship status, national origin, race, religion, sexual orientation, socioeconomic status). Behavior analysts also evaluate biases of their *supervisees* and *trainees,* as well as their supervisees' and trainees' ability to address the needs of individuals with diverse needs/backgrounds.

1.08 Nondiscrimination

Behavior analysts do not discriminate against others. They behave toward others in an equitable and inclusive manner regardless of age, disability, ethnicity, gender expression/identity, immigration status, marital/relationship status, national origin, race, religion, sexual orientation, socioeconomic status, or any other basis proscribed by law.

1.09 Nonharassment

Behavior analysts do not engage in behavior that is harassing or hostile toward others.

1.10 Awareness of Personal Biases and Challenges

Behavior analysts maintain awareness that their personal biases or challenges (e.g., mental or physical health conditions; legal, financial, marital/relationship challenges) may interfere with the effectiveness of their professional work. Behavior analysts take appropriate steps to resolve interference, ensure that their professional work is not compromised, and document all actions taken in this circumstance and the eventual outcomes.

1.11 Multiple Relationships

Because *multiple relationships* may result in a *conflict of interest* that might harm one or more parties, behavior analysts avoid entering into or creating multiple relationships, including professional, personal, and familial relationships with clients and colleagues. Behavior analysts communicate the risks of multiple relationships to relevant individuals and continually monitor for the development of multiple relationships. If multiple relationships arise, behavior analysts take appropriate steps to resolve them. When immediately resolving a multiple relationship is not possible, behavior analysts develop appropriate safeguards to identify and avoid conflicts of interest in compliance with the Code and develop a plan to eventually resolve the multiple relationship. Behavior analysts document all actions taken in this circumstance and the eventual outcomes.

1.12 Giving and Receiving Gifts
Because the exchange of gifts can invite conflicts of interest and multiple relationships, behavior analysts do not give gifts to or accept gifts from clients, *stakeholders, supervisees,* or *trainees* with a monetary value of more than $10 U.S. dollars (or the equivalent purchasing power in another currency). Behavior analysts make clients and stakeholders aware of this requirement at the onset of the professional relationship. A gift is acceptable if it functions as an infrequent expression of gratitude and does not result in financial benefit to the recipient. Instances of giving or accepting ongoing or cumulative gifts may rise to the level of a violation of this standard if the gifts become a regularly expected source of income or value to the recipient.

1.13 Coercive and Exploitative Relationships
Behavior analysts do not abuse their power or authority by coercing or exploiting persons over whom they have authority (e.g., evaluative, supervisory).

1.14 Romantic and Sexual Relationships
Behavior analysts do not engage in romantic or sexual relationships with current clients, stakeholders, trainees, or supervisees because such relationships pose a substantial risk of conflicts of interest and impaired judgment. Behavior analysts do not engage in romantic or sexual relationships with former clients or stakeholders for a minimum of two years from the date the professional relationship ended. Behavior analysts do not engage in romantic or sexual relationships with former supervisees or trainees until the parties can document that the professional relationship has ended (i.e., completion of all professional duties). Behavior analysts do not accept as supervisees or trainees individuals with whom they have had a past romantic or sexual relationship until at least six months after the relationship has ended.

1.15 Responding to Requests
Behavior analysts make appropriate efforts to respond to requests for information from and comply with deadlines of relevant individuals (e.g., clients, stakeholders, supervisees, trainees) and entities (e.g., BACB, licensure boards, funders). They also comply with practice requirements (e.g., attestations, criminal background checks) imposed by the BACB, employers, or governmental entities.

1.16 Self-Reporting Critical Information
Behavior analysts remain knowledgeable about and comply with all self-reporting requirements of relevant entities (e.g., BACB, licensure boards, funders).

SECTION 2—RESPONSIBILITY IN PRACTICE

2.01 Providing Effective Treatment
Behavior analysts prioritize *clients' rights* and needs in service delivery. They provide services that are conceptually consistent with behavioral principles, based on scientific evidence, and designed to maximize desired outcomes for and protect all *clients, stakeholders, supervisees, trainees,* and *research participants* from harm. Behavior analysts implement nonbehavioral services with clients only if they have the required education, formal training, and professional credentials to deliver such services.

2.02 Timeliness
Behavior analysts deliver services and carry out necessary service-related administrative responsibilities in a timely manner.

2.03 Protecting Confidential Information
Behavior analysts take appropriate steps to protect the confidentiality of clients, stakeholders, supervisees, trainees, and research participants; prevent the accidental or inadvertent sharing of confidential information; and comply with applicable confidentiality requirements (e.g., laws, regulations, organization policies). The scope of confidentiality includes service delivery (e.g., live, teleservices, recorded sessions); documentation and data; and verbal, written, or electronic communication.

2.04 Disclosing Confidential Information

Behavior analysts only share confidential information about clients, stakeholders, supervisees, trainees, or research participants: (1) when *informed consent* is obtained; (2) when attempting to protect the client or others from harm; (3) when attempting to resolve contractual issues; (4) when attempting to prevent a crime that is reasonably likely to cause physical, mental, or financial harm to another; or (5) when compelled to do so by law or court order. When behavior analysts are authorized to discuss confidential information with a *third party*, they only share information critical to the purpose of the communication.

2.05 Documentation Protection and Retention

Behavior analysts are knowledgeable about and comply with all applicable requirements (e.g., BACB rules, laws, regulations, contracts, funder and organization requirements) for storing, transporting, retaining, and destroying physical and electronic documentation related to their professional activities. They destroy physical documentation after making electronic copies or summaries of data (e.g., reports and graphs) only when allowed by applicable requirements. When a behavior analyst leaves an organization these responsibilities remain with the organization.

2.06 Accuracy in Service Billing and Reporting

Behavior analysts identify their services accurately and include all required information on reports, bills, invoices, requests for reimbursement, and receipts. They do not implement or bill nonbehavioral services under an authorization or contract for *behavioral services*. If inaccuracies in reporting or billing are discovered, they inform all relevant parties (e.g., organizations, licensure boards, funders), correct the inaccuracy in a timely manner, and document all actions taken in this circumstance and the eventual outcomes.

2.07 Fees

Behavior analysts implement fee practices and share fee information in compliance with applicable laws and regulations. They do not misrepresent their fees. In situations where behavior analysts are not directly responsible for fees, they must communicate these requirements to the responsible party and take steps to resolve any inaccuracy or conflict. They document all actions taken in this circumstance and the eventual outcomes.

2.08 Communicating About Services

Behavior analysts use understandable language in, and ensure comprehension of, all communications with clients, stakeholders, supervisees, trainees, and research participants. Before providing services, they clearly describe the scope of services and specify the conditions under which services will end. They explain all assessment and *behavior-change intervention* procedures before implementing them and explain assessment and intervention results when they are available. They provide an accurate and current set of their credentials and a description of their area of competence upon request.

2.09 Involving Clients and Stakeholders

Behavior analysts make appropriate efforts to involve clients and relevant stakeholders throughout the service relationship, including selecting goals, selecting and designing assessments and behavior-change interventions, and conducting continual progress monitoring.

2.10 Collaborating with Colleagues

Behavior analysts collaborate with colleagues from their own and other professions in the best interest of clients and stakeholders. Behavior analysts address conflicts by compromising when possible, but always prioritizing the best interest of the client. Behavior analysts document all actions taken in these circumstances and their eventual outcomes.

2.11 Obtaining Informed Consent

Behavior analysts are responsible for knowing about and complying with all conditions under which they are required to obtain informed consent from clients, stakeholders, and research participants (e.g., before initial implementation of assessments or behavior-change interventions, when making substantial changes to interventions, when exchanging or releasing confidential information or records). They are responsible for explaining, obtaining, reobtaining, and documenting required informed consent. They are responsible for obtaining assent from clients when applicable.

2.12 Considering Medical Needs

Behavior analysts ensure, to the best of their ability, that medical needs are assessed and addressed if there is any reasonable likelihood that a referred behavior is influenced by medical or biological variables. They document referrals made to a medical professional and follow up with the client after making the referral.

2.13 Selecting, Designing, and Implementing Assessments

Before selecting or designing behavior-change interventions behavior analysts select and design assessments that are conceptually consistent with behavioral principles; that are based on scientific evidence; and that best meet the diverse needs, context, and resources of the client and stakeholders. They select, design, and implement assessments with a focus on maximizing benefits and minimizing risk of harm to the client and stakeholders. They summarize the procedures and results in writing.

2.14 Selecting, Designing, and Implementing Behavior-Change Interventions

Behavior analysts select, design, and implement behavior-change interventions that: (1) are conceptually consistent with behavioral principles; (2) are based on scientific evidence; (3) are based on assessment results; (4) prioritize positive reinforcement procedures; and (5) best meet the diverse needs, context, and resources of the client and stakeholders. Behavior analysts also consider relevant factors (e.g., risks, benefits, and side effects; client and stakeholder preference; implementation efficiency; cost effectiveness) and design and implement behavior-change interventions to produce outcomes likely to maintain under naturalistic conditions. They summarize the behavior-change intervention procedures in writing (e.g., a behavior plan).

2.15 Minimizing Risk of Behavior-Change Interventions

Behavior analysts select, design, and implement behavior-change interventions (including the selection and use of consequences) with a focus on minimizing risk of harm to the client and stakeholders. They recommend and implement restrictive or punishment-based procedures only after demonstrating that desired results have not been obtained using less intrusive means, or when it is determined by an existing intervention team that the risk of harm to the client outweighs the risk associated with the behavior-change intervention. When recommending and implementing restrictive or punishment-based procedures, behavior analysts comply with any required review processes (e.g., a human rights review committee). Behavior analysts must continually evaluate and document the effectiveness of restrictive or punishment-based procedures and modify or discontinue the behavior-change intervention in a timely manner if it is ineffective.

2.16 Describing Behavior-Change Interventions Before Implementation

Before implementation, behavior analysts describe in writing the objectives and procedures of the behavior-change intervention, any projected timelines, and the schedule of ongoing review. They provide this information and explain the environmental conditions necessary for effective implementation of the behavior-change intervention to the stakeholders and client (when appropriate). They also provide explanations when modifying existing or introducing new behavior-change interventions and obtain informed consent when appropriate.

2.17 Collecting and Using Data

Behavior analysts actively ensure the appropriate selection and correct implementation of data collection procedures. They graphically display, summarize, and use the data to make decisions about continuing, modifying, or terminating services.

2.18 Continual Evaluation of the Behavior-Change Intervention

Behavior analysts engage in continual monitoring and evaluation of behavior-change interventions. If data indicate that desired outcomes are not being realized, they actively assess the situation and take appropriate corrective action. When a behavior analyst is concerned that services concurrently delivered by another professional are negatively impacting the behavior-change intervention, the behavior analyst takes appropriate steps to review and address the issue with the other professional.

2.19 Addressing Conditions Interfering with Service Delivery

Behavior analysts actively identify and address environmental conditions (e.g., the behavior of others, hazards to the client or staff, disruptions) that may interfere with or prevent service delivery. In such situations, behavior analysts remove or minimize the conditions, identify effective modifications to the intervention, and/or consider obtaining or recommending assistance from other professionals. Behavior analysts document the conditions, all actions taken, and the eventual outcomes.

SECTION 3—RESPONSIBILITY TO CLIENTS AND STAKEHOLDERS

3.01 Responsibility to Clients (see 1.03, 2.01)
Behavior analysts act in the best interest of *clients,* taking appropriate steps to support *clients' rights,* maximize benefits, and do no harm. They are also knowledgeable about and comply with applicable laws and regulations related to mandated reporting requirements.

3.02 Identifying Stakeholders
Behavior analysts identify *stakeholders* when providing services. When multiple stakeholders (e.g., parent or *legally authorized representative,* teacher, principal) are involved, the behavior analyst identifies their relative obligations to each stakeholder. They document and communicate those obligations to stakeholders at the outset of the professional relationship.

3.03 Accepting Clients (see 1.05, 1.06)
Behavior analysts only accept clients whose requested services are within their identified *scope of competence* and available resources (e.g., time and capacity for case supervision, staffing). When behavior analysts are directed to accept clients outside of their identified scope of competence and available resources, they take appropriate steps to discuss and resolve the concern with relevant parties. Behavior analysts document all actions taken in this circumstance and the eventual outcomes.

3.04 Service Agreement (see 1.04)
Before implementing services, behavior analysts ensure that there is a signed service agreement with the client and/or relevant stakeholders outlining the responsibilities of all parties, the scope of *behavioral services* to be provided, the behavior analyst's obligations under the Code, and procedures for submitting complaints about a behavior analyst's professional practices to relevant entities (e.g., BACB, service organization, licensure board, funder). They update service agreements as needed or as required by relevant parties (e.g., service organizations, licensure boards, funders). Updated service agreements must be reviewed with and signed by the client and/or relevant stakeholders.

3.05 Financial Agreements (see 1.04, 2.07)
Before beginning services, behavior analysts document agreed-upon compensation and billing practices with their clients, relevant stakeholders, and/or funders. When funding circumstances change, they must be revisited with these parties. Pro bono and bartered services are only provided under a specific service agreement and in compliance with the Code.

3.06 Consulting with Other Providers (see 1.05, 2.04, 2.10, 2.11, 2.12)
Behavior analysts arrange for appropriate consultation with and referrals to other providers in the best interests of their clients, with appropriate *informed consent,* and in compliance with applicable requirements (e.g., laws, regulations, contracts, organization and funder policies).

3.07 Third-Party Contracts for Services (see 1.04, 1.11, 2.04, 2.07)
When behavior analysts enter into a signed contract to provide services to a client at the request of a *third party* (e.g., school district, governmental entity), they clarify the nature of the relationship with each party and assess any potential conflicts before services begin. They ensure that the contract outlines (1) the responsibilities of all parties, (2) the scope of behavioral services to be provided, (3) the likely use of the information obtained, (4) the behavior analysts' obligations under the Code, and (5) any limits about maintaining confidentiality. Behavior analysts are responsible for amending contracts as needed and reviewing them with the relevant parties at that time.

3.08 Responsibility to the Client with Third-Party Contracts for Services (see 1.05, 1.11, 2.01)
Behavior analysts place the client's care and welfare above all others. If the third party requests services from the behavior analyst that are incompatible with the behavior analyst's recommendations, that are outside of the behavior analyst's scope of competence, or that could result in a *multiple relationship,* behavior analysts resolve

such conflicts in the best interest of the client. If a conflict cannot be resolved, the behavior analyst may obtain additional training or consultation, discontinue services following appropriate transition measures, or refer the client to another behavior analyst. Behavior analysts document all actions taken in this circumstance and the eventual outcomes.

3.09 Communicating with Stakeholders About Third-Party Contracted Services *(2.04, 2.08, 2.09, 2.11)*
When providing services at the request of a third party to a minor or individual who does not have the legal right to make personal decisions, behavior analysts ensure that the parent or legally authorized representative is informed of the rationale for and scope of services to be provided, as well as their right to receive copies of all service documentation and data. Behavior analysts are knowledgeable about and comply with all requirements related to informed consent, regardless of who requested the services.

3.10 Limitations of Confidentiality *(see 1.02, 2.03, 2.04)*
Behavior analysts inform clients and stakeholders of the limitations of confidentiality at the outset of the professional relationship and when information disclosures are required.

3.11 Documenting Professional Activity *(see 1.04, 2.03, 2.05, 2.06, 2.10)*
Throughout the service relationship, behavior analysts create and maintain detailed and high-quality documentation of their professional activities to facilitate provision of services by them or by other professionals, to ensure accountability, and to meet applicable requirements (e.g., laws, regulations, funder and organization policies). Documentation must be created and maintained in a manner that allows for timely communication and transition of services, should the need arise.

3.12 Advocating for Appropriate Services *(1.04, 1.05, 2.01, 2.08)*
Behavior analysts advocate for and educate clients and stakeholders about evidence-based assessment and *behavior-change intervention* procedures. They also advocate for the appropriate amount and level of behavioral service provision and oversight required to meet defined client goals.

3.13 Referrals *(see 1.05, 1.11, 2.01, 2.04, 2.10)*
Behavior analysts make referrals based on the needs of the client and/or relevant stakeholders and include multiple providers when available. Behavior analysts disclose to the client and relevant stakeholders any relationships they have with potential providers, and fees or incentives they may receive for the referrals. They document any referrals made, including relevant relationships and fees or incentives received, and make appropriate efforts to follow up with the client and/or relevant stakeholders.

3.14 Facilitating Continuity of Services *(see 1.03, 2.02, 2.05, 2,08, 2.10)*
Behavior analysts act in the best interests of the client to avoid interruption or disruption of services. They make appropriate and timely efforts to facilitate the continuation of behavioral services in the event of planned interruptions (e.g., relocation, temporary leave of absence) and unplanned interruptions (e.g., illness, funding disruption, parent request, emergencies). They ensure that service agreements or contracts include a general plan of action for service interruptions. When a service interruption occurs, they communicate to all relevant parties the steps being taken to facilitate continuity of services. Behavior analysts document all actions taken in this circumstance and the eventual outcomes.

3.15 Appropriately Discontinuing Services *(see 1.03, 2.02, 2.05. 2.10, 2.19)*
Behavior analysts include the circumstances for discontinuing services in their service agreement. They consider discontinuing services when: (1) the client has met all behavior-change goals, (2) the client is not benefiting from the service, (3) the behavior analyst and/or their *supervisees* or *trainees* are exposed to potentially harmful conditions that cannot be reasonably resolved, (4) the client and/or relevant stakeholder requests discontinuation, (5) the relevant stakeholders are not complying with the behavior-change intervention despite appropriate efforts to address barriers, or (6) services are no longer funded. Behavior analysts provide the client and/or relevant stakeholders with a written plan for discontinuing services, document acknowledgment of the plan, review the plan throughout the discharge process, and document all steps taken.

3.16 Appropriately Transitioning Services *(see 1.03, 2.02, 2.05. 2.10)*

Behavior analysts include in their service agreement the circumstances for transitioning the client to another behavior analyst within or outside of their organization. They make appropriate efforts to effectively manage transitions; provide a written plan that includes target dates, transition activities, and responsible parties; and review the plan throughout the transition. When relevant, they take appropriate steps to minimize disruptions to services during the transition by collaborating with relevant service providers.

SECTION 4—RESPONSIBILITY TO SUPERVISEES AND TRAINEES

4.01 Compliance with Supervision Requirements *(see 1.02)*

Behavior analysts are knowledgeable about and comply with all applicable supervisory requirements (e.g., BACB rules, licensure requirements, funder and organization policies), including those related to supervision modalities and structure (e.g., in person, video conference, individual, group).

4.02 Supervisory Competence *(see 1.05, 1.06)*

Behavior analysts supervise and train others only within their identified *scope of competence*. They provide supervision only after obtaining knowledge and skills in effective supervisory practices, and they continually evaluate and improve their supervisory repertoires through professional development.

4.03 Supervisory Volume *(see 1.02, 1.05, 2.01)*

Behavior analysts take on only the number of *supervisees* or *trainees* that allows them to provide effective supervision and training. They are knowledgeable about and comply with any relevant requirements (e.g., BACB rules, licensure requirements, funder and organization policies). They consider relevant factors (e.g., their current client demands, their current supervisee or trainee caseload, time and logistical resources) on an ongoing basis and when deciding to add a supervisee or trainee. When behavior analysts determine that they have met their threshold volume for providing effective supervision, they document this self-assessment and communicate the results to their employer or other relevant parties.

4.04 Accountability in Supervision *(see 1.03)*

Behavior analysts are accountable for their supervisory practices. They are also accountable for the professional activities (e.g., client services, supervision, training, research activity, public statements) of their supervisees or trainees that occur as part of the supervisory relationship.

4.05 Maintaining Supervision Documentation *(1.01, 1.02, 1.04, 2.03, 2.05, 3.11)*

Behavior analysts create, update, store, and dispose of documentation related to their supervisees or trainees by following all applicable requirements (e.g., BACB rules, licensure requirements, funder and organization policies), including those relating to confidentiality. They ensure that their documentation, and the documentation of their supervisees or trainees, is accurate and complete. They maintain documentation in a manner that allows for the effective transition of supervisory oversight if necessary. They retain their supervision documentation for at least 7 years and as otherwise required by law and other relevant parties and instruct their supervisees or trainees to do the same.

4.06 Providing Supervision and Training *(see 1.02, 1.13 2.01)*

Behavior analysts deliver supervision and training in compliance with applicable requirements (e.g., BACB rules, licensure requirements, funder and organization policies). They design and implement supervision and training procedures that are evidence based, focus on positive reinforcement, and are individualized for each supervisee or trainee and their circumstances.

4.07 Incorporating and Addressing Diversity *(see 1.05, 1.06, 1.07, 1.10)*

During supervision and training, behavior analysts actively incorporate and address topics related to diversity (e.g., age, disability, ethnicity, gender expression/identity, immigration status, marital/relationship status, national origin, race, religion, sexual orientation, socioeconomic status).

4.08 Performance Monitoring and Feedback *(see 2.02, 2.05, 2.17, 2.18)*

Behavior analysts engage in and document ongoing, evidence-based data collection and performance monitoring (e.g., observations, structured evaluations) of supervisees or trainees. They provide timely informal and formal praise and feedback designed to improve performance and document formal feedback delivered. When performance problems arise, behavior analysts develop, communicate, implement, and evaluate an improvement plan with clearly identified procedures for addressing the problem.

4.09 Delegation of Tasks (see 1.03)
Behavior analysts delegate tasks to their supervisees or trainees only after confirming that they can competently perform the tasks and that the delegation complies with applicable requirements (e.g., BACB rules, licensure requirements, funder and organization policies).

4.10 Evaluating Effects of Supervision and Training (see 1.03, 2.17, 2.18)
Behavior analysts actively engage in continual evaluation of their own supervisory practices using feedback from others and *client* and supervisee or trainee outcomes. Behavior analysts document those self-evaluations and make timely adjustments to their supervisory and training practices as indicated.

4.11 Facilitating Continuity of Supervision (see 1.03, 2.02, 3.14)
Behavior analysts minimize interruption or disruption of supervision and make appropriate and timely efforts to facilitate the continuation of supervision in the event of planned interruptions (e.g., temporary leave) or unplanned interruptions (e.g., illness, emergencies). When an interruption or disruption occurs, they communicate to all relevant parties the steps being taken to facilitate continuity of supervision

4.12 Appropriately Terminating Supervision (see 1.03, 2.02, 3.15)
When behavior analysts determine, for any reason, to terminate supervision or other services that include supervision, they work with all relevant parties to develop a plan for terminating supervision that minimizes negative impacts to the supervisee or trainee. They document all actions taken in this circumstance and the eventual outcomes.

SECTION 5—RESPONSIBILITY IN PUBLIC STATEMENTS

5.01 Protecting the Rights of Clients, Stakeholders, Supervisees, and Trainees (see 1.03, 3.01)
Behavior analysts take appropriate steps to protect the *rights* of their *clients, stakeholders, supervisees,* and *trainees* in all *public statements.* Behavior analysts prioritize the rights of their clients in all public statements.

5.02 Confidentiality in Public Statements (see 2.03, 2.04, 3.10)
In all public statements, behavior analysts protect the confidentiality of their clients, supervisees, and trainees, except when allowed. They make appropriate efforts to prevent accidental or inadvertent sharing of confidential or identifying information.

5.03 Public Statements by Behavior Analysts (see 1.01, 1.02)
When providing public statements about their professional activities, or those of others with whom they are affiliated, behavior analysts take reasonable precautions to ensure that the statements are truthful and do not mislead or exaggerate either because of what they state, convey, suggest, or omit; and are based on existing research and a behavioral conceptualization. Behavior analysts do not provide specific advice related to a client's needs in public forums.

5.04 Public Statements by Others (see 1.03)
Behavior analysts are responsible for public statements that promote their professional activities or products, regardless of who creates or publishes the statements. Behavior analysts make reasonable efforts to prevent others (e.g., employers, marketers, clients, stakeholders) from making deceptive statements concerning their professional activities or products. If behavior analysts learn of such statements, they make reasonable efforts to correct them. Behavior analysts document all actions taken in this circumstance and the eventual outcomes.

5.05 Use of Intellectual Property (see 1.01, 1.02, 1.03)
Behavior analysts are knowledgeable about and comply with intellectual property laws, including obtaining permission to use materials that have been trademarked or copyrighted or can otherwise be claimed as another's intellectual property as defined by law. Appropriate use of such materials includes providing citations,

attributions, and/or trademark or copyright symbols. Behavior analysts do not unlawfully obtain or disclose proprietary information, regardless of how it became known to them.

5.06 Advertising Nonbehavioral Services *(see 1.01, 1.02, 2.01)*

Behavior analysts do not advertise nonbehavioral services as *behavioral services*. If behavior analysts provide nonbehavioral services, those services must be clearly distinguished from their behavioral services and BACB certification with the following disclaimer: "These interventions are not behavioral in nature and are not covered by my BACB certification." This disclaimer is placed alongside the names and descriptions of all nonbehavioral interventions. If a behavior analyst is employed by an organization that violates this Code standard, the behavior analyst makes reasonable efforts to remediate the situation, documenting all actions taken and the eventual outcomes.

5.07 Soliciting Testimonials from Current Clients for Advertising *(see 1.11, 1.13, 2.11, 3.01, 3.10)*

Because of the possibility of undue influence and implicit coercion, behavior analysts do not solicit *testimonials* from current clients or stakeholders for use in advertisements designed to obtain new clients. This does not include unsolicited reviews on *websites* where behavior analysts cannot control content, but such content should not be used or shared by the behavior analyst. If a behavior analyst is employed by an organization that violates this Code standard, the behavior analyst makes reasonable efforts to remediate the situation, documenting all actions taken and the eventual outcomes.

5.08 Using Testimonials from Former Clients for Advertising *(see 2.03, 2.04, 2.11, 3.01, 3.10)*

When soliciting testimonials from former clients or stakeholders for use in advertisements designed to obtain new clients, behavior analysts consider the possibility that former clients may re-enter services. These testimonials must be identified as solicited or unsolicited, include an accurate statement of the relationship between the behavior analyst and the testimonial author, and comply with all applicable privacy and confidentiality laws. When soliciting testimonials from former clients or stakeholders, behavior analysts provide them with clear and thorough descriptions about where and how the testimonial will appear, make them aware of any risks associated with the disclosure of their private information, and inform them that they can rescind the testimonial at any time. If a behavior analyst is employed by an organization that violates this Code standard, the behavior analyst makes reasonable efforts to remediate the situation, documenting all actions taken and the eventual outcomes.

5.09 Using Testimonials for Nonadvertising Purposes *(see 1.02, 2.03. 2.04, 2.11, 3.01, 3.10)*

Behavior analysts may use testimonials from former or current clients and stakeholders for nonadvertising purposes (e.g., fundraising, grant applications, dissemination of information about ABA) in accordance with applicable laws. If a behavior analyst is employed by an organization that violates this Code standard, the behavior analyst makes reasonable efforts to remediate the situation, documenting all actions taken and the eventual outcomes.

5.10 Social Media Channels and Websites *(see 1.02, 2.03, 2.04, 2.11, 3.01, 3.10)*

Behavior analysts are knowledgeable about the risks to privacy and confidentiality associated with the use of *social media channels* and websites and they use their respective professional and personal accounts accordingly. They do not publish information and/or *digital content* of clients on their **personal** social media accounts and websites. When publishing information and/or digital content of clients on their **professional** social media accounts and websites, behavior analysts ensure that for each publication they (1) obtain *informed consent* before publishing, (2) include a disclaimer that informed consent was obtained and that the information should not be captured and reused without express permission, (3) publish on social media channels in a manner that reduces the potential for sharing, and (4) make appropriate efforts to prevent and correct misuse of the shared information, documenting all actions taken and the eventual outcomes. Behavior analysts frequently monitor their social media accounts and websites to ensure the accuracy and appropriateness of shared information.

5.11 *Using Digital Content in Public Statements* (see 1.02, 1.03, 2.03, 2.04, 2.11, 3.01, 3.10)

Before publicly sharing information about clients using digital content, behavior analysts ensure confidentiality, obtain informed consent before sharing, and only use the content for the intended purpose and audience. They ensure that all shared media is accompanied by a disclaimer indicating that informed consent was obtained. If a behavior analyst is employed by an organization that violates this Code standard, the behavior analyst makes reasonable efforts to remediate the situation, documenting all actions taken and the eventual outcomes.

SECTION 6—RESPONSIBILITY IN RESEARCH

6.01 *Conforming with Laws and Regulations in Research* (see 1.02)

Behavior analysts plan and conduct *research* in a manner consistent with all applicable laws and regulations, as well as requirements by organizations and institutions governing research activity.

6.02 *Research Review* (see 1.02, 1.04, 3.01)

Behavior analysts conduct research, whether independent of or in the context of service delivery, only after approval by a formal *research review committee.*

6.03 *Research in Service Delivery* (see 1.02, 1.04, 2.01, 3.01)

Behavior analysts conducting research in the context of service delivery must arrange research activities such that *client* services and client welfare are prioritized. In these situations, behavior analysts must comply with all ethics requirements for both service delivery and research within the Code. When professional services are offered as an incentive for research participation, behavior analysts clarify the nature of the services, and any potential risks, obligations, and limitations for all parties.

6.04 *Informed Consent in Research* (see 1.04, 2.08, 2.11)

Behavior analysts are responsible for obtaining *informed consent* (and assent when relevant) from potential *research participants* under the conditions required by the research review committee. When behavior analysts become aware that data obtained from past or current clients, *stakeholders, supervisees,* and/or *trainees* during typical service delivery might be disseminated to the scientific community, they obtain informed consent for use of the data before dissemination, specify that services will not be impacted by providing or withholding consent, and make available the right to withdraw consent at any time without penalty.

6.05 *Confidentiality in Research* (see 2.03, 2.04, 2.05)

Behavior analysts prioritize the confidentiality of their research participants except under conditions where it may not possible. They make appropriate efforts to prevent accidental or inadvertent sharing of confidential or identifying information while conducting research and in any dissemination activity related to the research (e.g., disguising or removing confidential or identifying information).

6.06 *Competence in Conducting Research* (see 1.04, 1.05, 1.06, 3.01)

Behavior analysts only conduct research independently after they have successfully conducted research under a supervisor in a defined relationship (e.g., thesis, dissertation, mentored research project). Behavior analysts and their assistants are permitted to perform only those research activities for which they are appropriately trained and prepared. Before engaging in research activities for which a behavior analyst has not received training, they seek the appropriate training and become demonstrably competent or they collaborate with other professionals who have the required competence. Behavior analysts are responsible for the ethical conduct of all personnel assigned to the research project.

6.07 *Conflict of Interest in Research and Publication* (see 1.01, 1.11, 1.13)

When conducting research, behavior analysts identify, disclose, and address *conflicts of interest* (e.g., personal, financial, organization related, service related). They also identify, disclose, and address conflicts of interest in their publication and editorial activities.

6.08 Appropriate Credit *(see 1.01, 1.11, 1.13)*

Behavior analysts give appropriate credit (e.g., authorship, author-note acknowledgment) to research contributors in all dissemination activities. Authorship and other publication acknowledgments accurately reflect the relative scientific or professional contributions of the individuals involved, regardless of their professional status (e.g., professor, student).

6.09 Plagiarism *(see 1.01)*

Behavior analysts do not present portions or elements of another's work or data as their own. Behavior analysts only republish their previously published data or text when accompanied by proper disclosure.

6.10 Documentation and Data Retention in Research *(see 2.03, 2.05, 3.11, 4.05)*

Behavior analysts must be knowledgeable about and comply with all applicable standards (e.g., BACB rules, laws, research review committee requirements) for storing, transporting, retaining, and destroying physical and electronic documentation related to research. They retain identifying documentation and data for the longest required duration. Behavior analysts destroy physical documentation after making deidentified digital copies or summaries of data (e.g., reports and graphs) when permitted by relevant entities.

6.11 Accuracy and Use of Data *(see 1.01, 2.17, 5.03)*

Behavior analysts do not fabricate data or falsify results in their research, publications, and presentations. They plan and carry out their research and describe their procedures and findings to minimize the possibility that their research and results will be misleading or misinterpreted. If they discover errors in their published data they take steps to correct them by following publisher policy. Data from research projects are presented to the public and scientific community in their entirety whenever possible. When that is not possible, behavior analysts take caution and explain the exclusion of data (whether single data points, or partial or whole data sets) from presentations or manuscripts submitted for publication by providing a rationale and description of what was excluded.

Appendix B: Suggestions for Related Ethics Codes

Please remember, while the authors of this workbook have included suggestions of codes in relation to the provided scenarios, additional or alternative codes may be associated with the identified situation. The codes indicated may represent clear violations or may be related to the scenario as presented and may be appropriate for further review. Recommended codes are the opinion of the authors. Readers are encouraged to first consider all options and form their own interpretations and impressions. While the codes highlighted below for review may be regarded as potentially the most relevant, discussion, interpretation, and evaluation of the scenario may not only increase the utility of this workbook in developing skill and proficiency in ethical decision-making and analysis but also yield identification of diverse codes.

SECTION 1: RESPONSIBILITY AS A PROFESSIONAL

Case 1: Signed, Sealed—Review Code(s): 1.01; 1.02
Case 2: Licensed to Ill—Review Code(s): 1.02
Case 3: Dropped Deadline—1.03; 2.02
Case 4: Divided Attention—1.04
Case 5: Parents' Night Out—1.04
Case 6: Risky Referral—1.05; 3.03
Case 7: Learn Something New—1.05
Case 8: Above Paygrade—1.05
Case 9: ACTing Ethically—1.05
Case 10: Is There a Doctor in the House?—1.05
Case 11: How Different Can It Be?—1.05
Case 12: Requested Removal—1.07; 1.08
Case 13: Human Resources—1.08; 1.09
Case 14: Discrimination Discrepancy—1.08; 1.07
Case 15: Equal Opportunity—1.08; 1.07
Case 16: Cultural Conclusions—1.08
Case 17: Canceled Considerations—1.07
Case 18: Break Up, Break Down—1.10
Case 19: Request for Service—1.11
Case 20: Unfriend Request—1.11
Case 21: Party Time—1.11
Case 22: The Only One for the Job—1.11
Case 23: Someone's Gotta Do It—1.11
Case 24: I Know That Guy—1.11
Case 25: Lack of Snack—1.12; 1.07
Case 26: Ethical Headache—1.12
Case 27: Sharing Is Caring—1.12
Case 28: Season Pass—1.12
Case 29: More Than Friends—1.14
Case 30: Swipe Left—1.14

SECTION 2: RESPONSIBILITY IN PRACTICE

SECTION 3: RESPONSIBILITY TO CLIENTS AND STAKEHOLDERS

SECTION 4: RESPONSIBILITY TO SUPERVISEES AND TRAINEES

SECTION 5: RESPONSIBILITY IN PUBLIC STATEMENTS

SECTION 6: RESPONSIBILITY IN RESEARCH

COMPLEX SCENARIOS INVOLVING MULTIPLE SECTIONS OF THE CODE

Case 108: No Show, Oh No!—1.01; 1.03; 2.06; 4.04
Case 109: Splitting Up Is Hard to Do—1.11; 2.19
Case 110: Academic Advocacy—2.01; 2.10; 2.19; 3.08; 3.12
Case 111: Something's in the Air—2.01; 3.12
Case 112: Bury the Lead—2.06; 3.11
Case 113: Chosen Name—2.09; 1.08; 1.07
Case 114: My Way or the Highway—2.19; 3.15; 3.16
Case 115: Sign on the Dotted Line—4.04; 1.01; 1.03; 2.06
Case 116: Lost in Translation—1.07; 2.19; 2.08; 2.09
Case 117: Mad Scientist—6.04; 6.03; 4.06; 4.01; 1.13; 1.01
Case 118: Social Media Mayday—1.04; 1.09; 2.13; 5.03
Case 119: Wear Many Hats—2.01; 2.06; 5.06; 1.11
Case 120: Need for Concern?—2.04; 3.01; 2.19
Case 121: Glitch—1.03; 2.06
Case 122: Behind Closed Doors—3.01; 2.15; 2.09
Case 123: Adapt and Adjust—2.12; 3.06; 2.17

REFERENCES

American Psychological Association. (2018). *Potential ethical violations.* http://www.apa.org/topics/ethics/potential-violations.asp.

Baer, D. D., Wolf, M. M., & Risley, T. R. (1968). Some current dimensions of applied behavior analysis. *Journal of Applied Behavior Analysis, 1*, 91–97. https://doi.org/10.1901/jaba.1968.1-91.

Bailey, J., & Burch, M. (2016). *Ethics for behavior analysts* (3rd ed.). Taylor & Francis. https://doi.org/10.4324/9781315669212.

Behavior Analyst Certification Board. (n.d.). BACB certificant data. https://www.bacb.com/BACB-certificant-data.

Behavior Analyst Certification Board. (2014). *Behavior analyst certification board professional and ethical compliance code for behavior analysts.* https://www.bacb.com/wp-content/uploads/2017/09/170706-compliance-code-english.pdf.

Behavior Analyst Certification Board. (2017). *BCBA task list* (5th ed.). https://www.bacb.com/wp-content/uploads/2020/08/BCBA-task-list-5th-ed-210202.pdf.

Behavior Analyst Certification Board. (2018). *A summary of ethics violations and code-enforcement activities: 2016–2017.* https://www.bacb.com/wp-content/uploads/2020/05/180606_CodeEnforcementSummary.pdf.

Behavior Analyst Certification Board. (2020a). *BCaBA task list* (5th ed.). https://www.bacb.com/wp-content/uploads/2020/08/BCaBA-task-list-5th-ed-210202.pdf.

Behavior Analyst Certification Board. (2020b). *Ethics code for behavior analysts.* https://www.bacb.com/wp-content/uploads/2020/11/Ethics-Code-for-Behavior-Analysts-2102010.pdf.

Behavior Analyst Certification Board. (2021). *RBT ethics code (2.0).* https://www.bacb.com/wp-content/uploads/2020/05/RBT-Ethics-Code_190227.pdf.

Britton, L. N., Crye, A. A., & Haymes, L. K. (2021). Cultivating the ethical repertoires of behavior analysts: Prevention of common violations. *Behavior Analysis in Practice, 14*, 534–548. https://doi.org/10.1007/s40617-020-00540-w.

Brodhead, M. T. (2015). Maintaining professional relationships in an interdisciplinary setting: Strategies for navigating nonbehavioral treatment recommendations for individuals with autism. *Behavior Analysis in Practice, 8*, 70–78. https://doi.org/10.1007/s40617-015-0042-7.

Brodhead, M. T. (2019). Culture always matters: Some thoughts on Rosenberg and Schwartz. *Behavior Analysis in Practice, 12*, 826–830. https://doi.org/10.1007/s40617-019-00351-8.

Brodhead, M. T., Cox, D. J., & Quigley, S. P. (2018a). *Practical ethics for effective treatment of autism spectrum disorder.* Elsevier. https://doi.org/10.1016/b978-0-12-814098-7.00009-2.

Brodhead, M. T., & Higbee, T. S. (2012). Teaching and maintaining ethical behavior in a professional organization. *Behavior Analysis in Practice, 5*, 82–88. https://doi.org/10.1007/bf03391827.

Brodhead, M. T., Quigley, S. P., & Wilczynski, S. M. (2018b). A call for discussion about scope of competence in behavior analysis. *Behavior Analysis in Practice, 11*, 424–435. https://doi.org/10.1007/s40617-018-00303-8.

Cooper, J. O., Heron, T. E., & Heward, W. L. (2020). *Applied behavior analysis* (3rd ed.). Pearson/Merrill-Prentice Hall.

Cox, D. J. (2020). A guide to establishing ethics committees in behavioral health settings. *Behavior Analysis in Practice, 13*, 939–949. https://doi.org/10.31234/osf.io/br67g.

Dawson, M. (2004). *The misbehaviour of behaviourists: Ethical challenges to the autism-ABA industry.* http://www.sentex.net/~nexus23/naa_aba.html.

Dorsey, M. F., Weinberg, M., Zane, T., & Guidi, M. M. (2007). The case for licensure of applied behavior analysts. *Behavior Analysis in Practice, 2*, 53–58. https://doi.org/10.1007/bf03391738.

Finn, P., Bothe, A. K., & Bramlett, R. E. (2005). Science and pseudoscience in communication disorders: Criteria and applications. *American Journal of Speech-Language Pathology, 14*, 172–186. https://doi.org/10.1044/1058-0360(2005/018).

Fong, E. H., Catagnus, R. M., Brodhead, M. T., Quigley, S., & Field, S. (2016). Developing the cultural awareness skills of behavior analysts. *Behavior Analysis in Practice, 9*, 84–94. https://doi.org/10.1007/s40617-016-0111-6.

Fong, E. H., & Tanaka, S. (2013). Multicultural alliance of behavior analysis standards for cultural competence in behavior analysis. *International Journal of Behavioral Consultation and Therapy, 8*(2), 17–19. https://doi.org/10.1037/h0100970.

Forester-Miller, H., & Davis, T. E. (2016). *Practitioner's guide to ethical decision making* (rev. ed.). https://www.counseling.org/docs/default-source/ethics/practitioner-39-s-guide-to-ethical-decision-making.pdf.

Gershfeld Litvak, S., & Sush, D. J. (in press). Ethics & legal issues. In J. L. Matson (Ed.), Applied behavior analysis: A comprehensive handbook. Springer.

Ghezzi, P., & Rehfeldt, R. (1994). Competence. In L. J. Hayes, S. C. Hayes, G. J. Moore, & P. M. Ghezzi (Eds.), *Ethical issues in developmental disabilities* (pp. 81–88). Context Press.

Handelsman, M. M. (1986). Problems with ethics training by "osmosis". *Professional Psychology: Research and Practice*, *17*, 371–372. https://doi.org/10.1037/0735-7028.17.4.371.

Kelly, M. P., Martin, N., Dillenburger, K., Kelly, A. N., & Miller, M. M. (2019). Spreading the news: History, successes, challenges and the ethics of effective dissemination. *Behavior Analysis in Practice, 12*(2), 440–451. https://doi.org/10.1007/s40617-018-0238-8.

Leaf, J. B., Cihon, J. H., Leaf, R., McEachin, J., Liu, N., Russell, N., et al. (2021). Concerns about ABA-based intervention: An evaluation and recommendations. *Journal of Autism and Developmental Disorders*, 1–16. https://doi.org/10.1007/s10803-021-05200-8.

LeBlanc, L. A., Onofrio, O. M., Valentino, A. L., & Sleeper, J. D. (2020a). Promoting ethical discussions and decision making in a human service agency. *Behavior Analysis in Practice, 13*, 905–913. https://doi.org/10.1007/s40617-020-00454-7.

LeBlanc, L. A., Sellers, T. P., & Ala'i, S. (2020b). *Building and sustaining meaningful and effective relationships as a supervisor and mentor*. Sloan Publishing.

Luiselli, J. K. (2015). In response: Maintaining professional relationships in an interdisciplinary setting: Strategies for navigating nonbehavioral treatment recommendations for individuals with autism. *Behavior Analysis in Practice, 8*, 79. https://doi.org/10.1007/s40617-015-0043-6.

National Autism Center. (2009, 2015). *National standards project*. http://www.nationalautismcenter.org/national-standards-project/.

Newhouse-Oisten, M. K., Peck, K. M., Conway, A. A., & Frieder, J. E. (2017). Ethical considerations for interdisciplinary collaboration with prescribing professionals. *Behavior Analysis in Practice, 10*, 145–153. https://doi.org/10.1007/s40617-017-0184-x.

O'Leary, P. N., Miller, M. M., Olive, M. L., & Kelly, A. N. (2017). Blurred lines: Ethical implications of social media for behavior analysts. *Behavior Analysis in Practice, 10*(1), 45–51. https://doi.org/10.1007/s40617-014-0033-0.

Phu, W., & Byrne, T. (2018). Testimonials on the web: Evidence for violations of the professional and ethical compliance code for behavior analysts. *Behavior Analysis: Research and Practice, 18*, 419–424. https://doi.org/10.1037/bar0000135.

Rosenberg, N. E., & Schwartz, I. S. (2019). Guidance or compliance: What makes an ethical behavior analyst? *Behavior Analysis in Practice, 12*, 473–482. https://doi.org/10.1007/s40617-018-00287-5.

Schlinger, H. D. (2015). Training graduate students to effectively disseminate behavior analysis and to counter misrepresentations. *Behavior Analysis in Practice, 8*, 110–112. https://doi.org/10.1007/s40617-014-0028-x.

Sellers, T. P., Alai-Rosales, S., & MacDonald, R. P. (2016a). Taking full responsibility: The ethics of supervision in behavior analytic practice. *Behavior Analysis in Practice, 9*, 299–308. https://doi.org/10.1007/s40617-016-0144-x.

Sellers, T. P., Carr, J. E., & Nosik, M. R. (2020). On the BACB's ethics requirements: A response to Rosenberg and Schwartz (2019). *Behavior Analysis in Practice, 13*, 714–717. https://doi.org/10.1007/s40617-020-00463-6.

Sellers, T. P., LeBlanc, L. A., & Valentino, A. L. (2016b). Recommendations for detecting and addressing barriers to successful supervision. *Behavior Analysis in Practice, 9*, 309–319. https://doi.org/10.1007/s40617-016-0142-z.

Sellers, T. P., Valentino, A. L., & LeBlanc, L. A. (2016c). Recommended practices for individual supervision of aspiring behavior analysts. *Behavior Analysis in Practice, 9*, 247–286. https://doi.org/10.1007/s40617-016-0110-7.

Smith, D. (2003). 10 ways practitioners can avoid frequent ethical pitfalls. *Monitor, 34*(1), 50. http://www.apa.org/monitor/jan03/10ways.aspx.

Smith, T., & Wick, J. (2008). Controversial treatments. In K. Chawarska, A. Klin, & F. R. Volkmar (Eds.), *Autism spectrum disorders in infants and toeddlers* (pp. 251–267). The Guilford Press.

Tarbox, J., Najdowski, A. C., & Lanagan, T. M. (2011). Behavioral observation and measurement. In J. Luiselli (Ed.), *Teaching and behavior support for children and adults with autism spectrum disorder: A practitioner's guide* (pp. 5–12). Oxford University Press, Inc.

Taylor, B. A., LeBlanc, L. A., & Nosik, M. R. (2019). Compassionate care in behavior analytic treatment: Can outcomes be enhanced by attending to relationships with caregivers? *Behavior Analysis in Practice, 12*, 654–666. https://doi.org/10.1007/s40617-018-00289-3.

Zane, T., Davis, C., & Rosswurm, M. (2008). The cost of fad treatments in autism. *Journal of Early and Intensive Behavior Intervention, 5*(2), 44–51. https://doi.org/10.1037/h0100418.

INDEX

Note: Page numbers followed by *f* indicate figures.

Printed in the USA
CPSIA information can be obtained
at www.ICGtesting.com
LVHW080215310724
786955LV00036B/1106